D1488902

# THE SPREAD OF ITALIAN HUMANISM

## MODERN LANGUAGES AND LITERATURE

*Literature Editor*

J. M. COHEN

# The Spread of Italian Humanism

**R. WEISS**

*Professor of Italian in the University of London*

HUTCHINSON UNIVERSITY LIBRARY

LONDON

HUTCHINSON & CO. (*Publishers*) LTD
*178–202 Great Portland Street, London, W.1*

London Melbourne Sydney
Auckland Bombay Toronto
Johannesburg New York

*First published 1964*

*This book has been set in Times New Roman type
face. It has been printed in Great Britain by The
Anchor Press, Ltd., in Tiptree, Essex, on Smooth
Wove paper*

To
Victoria Mary Geraldine Weiss

# Contents

# Preface

This book neither deals nor intends to deal with every aspect of the Renaissance in Western Europe. Its aim is instead to give a concise account of, or perhaps, to be more exact, an introduction to the literary side of the Renaissance in Italy and its impact on other literatures in the West of Europe. It offers the student a first acquaintance with a subject which can be pursued further by following the suggestions for more detailed reading in the bibliography. What the student is shown in this small book is how the outlook and the new literary forms of Renaissance Italy crossed the Alps and made themselves felt in France, England, Germany, Spain, and Portugal; and also how some Italian writers exerted an influence of fundamental importance on the literatures of these countries.

Any historical work must impose upon itself some chronological limits, and, so far as this book is concerned, the Renaissance is considered as ending about the middle of the sixteenth century. Needless to say, this is not an altogether satisfactory date, but it is doubtful whether any other date would have proved more convenient. As I have already said, and now repeat, my aim here is to give an introductory account of the Renaissance in Western European literature, not to give a literary history of the period. Accordingly the reader will find many important Renaissance writers not mentioned at all, while less important ones have been taken into consideration because of some especially significant characteristics in their work.

## PREFACE

I would like to conclude this brief introduction by express-
ing my grateful thanks to Mr J. M. Cohen and Mr J. D.
Moores for their many helpful suggestions, and to Miss
Anne Barthels for typing the manuscript of this book.

*University College London*

# I

# The beginnings of the Renaissance

THE Renaissance was the creation of nineteenth-century historians. The vision of the Renaissance which we have today remains on the whole that of men like Jacob Burckhardt and John Addington Symonds. It is true that research has found both these authors inadequate, yet the general impression they convey of a sudden change in practically every branch of culture—as if overnight the inhabitants of Florence, Venice, and Rome, not to mention other Italian towns, had decided to leave the Middle Ages behind and initiate what we now call the Renaissance—still remains with the layman.

This is far from the truth. Instead of a sudden revolution the Renaissance was the outcome of a slow, steady development; yet, though it is noticeable in many fields of human activity, it by no means shows a uniform rate of advance. The universities of Italy, and indeed of the whole of Western Europe, were in the main still medieval and Aristotle-ridden at the time when the rich flowering of painting and sculpture in Italy was degenerating into that mannerism which was the precursor of the Baroque.

Historians remind us that there were other renaissances besides the one which took place in Italy. There was one in the Carolingian age, another under the Othonian emperors, and yet another in twelfth-century France. We find a renaissance of the study of Roman Law, again in the twelfth century, and an Aristotelian renaissance during the thirteenth. Nevertheless, when we say 'Renaissance' without any qualification we mean the one which occurred in Italy during the fifteenth and sixteenth centuries.

The Italian Renaissance manifested itself in many directions—in the figurative arts, in architecture, in a new adventurousness of mind which made possible the discovery of America and other distant lands. In astronomy it is typified by Copernicus, whose studies at Padua and Bologna resulted in the dethronement of the heliocentric system of Ptolemy; in history it eliminated Providence as a factor in the shaping of human events, while with Machiavelli political treatises ceased to be at the same time handbooks of morals. However, it is not with any of these manifestations that I intend to deal but with the literary Renaissance; that is to say, Italian literature (whether in Latin or in the vernacular) and its impact on Western Europe.

Italian Renaissance literature was stimulated by the new emphasis on classical studies known as humanism. Both the classics themselves and humanism made their influence felt throughout Western Europe and changed its intellectual complexion. They were instrumental not only in creating new literary forms but also in revising modes of expression and replacing stale medieval rhetoric (which outside Italy still dragged on into the early sixteenth century) with something fresh and new and exciting. The resulting modernization of European literature was one of the greatest achievements of humanism.

The word 'humanism' was adopted by nineteenth-century historians to denote the revival of classical learning which revealed itself in Italy in the days of Petrarch. But in fact the Latin word 'humanista' and its Italian equivalent 'umanista' were already current in the literary world during the late fifteenth century, although with a different meaning. In Renaissance usage 'humanist' meant simply 'a teacher of Latin grammar'. It is true to say that many of the scholars whom we now call humanists also taught the humanities; in fact, in Italy during the fifteenth century they practically monopolized this field. But their teaching, their very vision of the world, was coloured by a new conception of classical antiquity, so much so that some of them came to think that their own way of life conformed to that of the ancient Romans. In reality, of course, an absolute barrier separated the humanists from their Roman ancestors. It was not that so many centuries had elapsed since the end of classical antiquity (when it actually ended is a matter of some dispute) but rather that, whether they liked it or not, they were divorced from it by the legacy of Christianity. However 'classical' they claimed or believed themselves to be, they merely achieved a classicism tempered by the beliefs, fears, prejudices, and aspirations of the Christian society in which they lived and had been brought up. Even the so-called 'paganism' of some humanists was never more than superficial; and if a few of them were hostile to Christianity this was not because they seriously dreamed of a revival of the old gods but because they were atheists (and atheists have existed in every age). They were never anything but a very small minority, in any case; and against such humanists as Platina or Leto, neither of whom had much use for the Christian religion, one can set others like Vegio, Traversari, or Battista Mantovano, who were beatified by the Church.

None the less, though not pagan, humanism in Italy remained fundamentally secular, just as Italian culture had been fundamentally lay during the Middle Ages. It was a different matter with humanism north of the Alps, where just as medieval learning had been a clerical monopoly so humanism was mainly Christian. Germany provided the only exception. Here, lay and Christian humanism flourished side by side and, when directed towards biblical studies, furnished the intellectual foundation of the Reformation. In fact, the Reformation advocated a return, much as humanism did, to origins, the primitive Church being its Greece and Rome.

It would be difficult to say exactly when humanism started in Italy. There is no clear distinction between what we understand now as humanism and those activities in the field of Latin studies which, despite the so-called 'dark ages', never really ceased during the Middle Ages. It is rather less difficult to see what first stimulated the rise of humanism in Italy. The emphasis on rhetorical studies in twelfth- and thirteenth-century Italy, and the twelfth-century revival of the study of Roman Law at Bologna, which really implied a return to classical sources, were partly responsible for the new turn taken by classical studies in some parts of Italy during the late thirteenth century. But this was by no means the whole story. New developments in trade and increased economic prosperity were responsible for a considerable degree of political and social change in fourteenth-century Italy. The Latin classics were no longer the virtual monopoly of cathedral and monastic libraries, and private persons came to own books not needed for strictly professional use. Lastly, the renewed study of Aristotle (who mainly through the advocacy of St. Thomas Aquinas almost acquired the prestige of a Church Father) may have stimulated a new and deeper approach to the study of the Latin classics—the Latin ones, since it was only during the fifteenth century that humanism seriously turned to Greek.

The first faint signs of humanism may be detected in the north Italian town of Padua during the second half of the thirteenth century. The final defeat and death in 1259 of Ezzelino III da Romano, the despicable tyrant who was still remembered with horror in the days of Ariosto, had delivered Padua from a nightmare and given the city a chance to flourish under its communal regime. It was here that the judge Lovato (1241–1309) inaugurated a novel approach to the Latin classics. His epistles in Latin verse, though belonging to a genre which had not been forgotten by medieval Latin writers, possess a new quality. For his predecessors the letter of the classics had been good enough. It was quite plainly not good enough for him: clearly he sought to capture the spirit of his models as well. On the whole he remained imprisoned within the Gothic structure of his age. Yet he made remarkable efforts to force his way out of the prevailing subservience to rhetoric and come closer to the outlook of the Latin classics.

As a classical scholar, Lovato was particularly fortunate. The number of ancient writers known and read during the later Middle Ages was not large. It is true that Virgil, Horace, Ovid, Lucan, Statius, Seneca, Cicero, and Sallust were assiduously read. But writers of primary importance like Catullus, Tacitus, Lucretius, and the Younger Pliny, as well as much of Livy and Cicero, had been forgotten for centuries, either because they were too difficult or because their works were too bulky, or because they were not considered useful. Lovato gained access to one of the greatest treasure-houses of classical manuscripts in Italy, the library of the Abbey of Pomposa. He circulated his 'finds' among his friends, with the result that by the end of the thirteenth century Paduan scholars could boast an unrivalled knowledge of classical Latin poetry. Lovato was a man of law, and he never taught. But he had a genius for friendship and enough personality to dominate the intellectual life of his town. He identified a skeleton, which came to light during the digging of the foundations of a hospital, as the remains of the Trojan Antenor, then believed to have been the founder of Padua, and his identification remained unchallenged until the high Renaissance. Again, his unravelling of the obscure metric rules governing the versification of Seneca's tragedies led to a fashion for these plays in Padua which lasted for at least a couple of generations.

Lovato's achievement, his personal authority, and his prestige as a writer of Latin verse, influenced his own nephew, the judge Rolando da Piazzola (1260–1330). His Latin orations and antiquarian tastes plainly bear his uncle's hallmark. Another Paduan judge, about ten or fifteen years younger than Lovato, Geremia da Montagnone (c.1255–1321), preferred to indulge in the medieval pastime of collecting quotations from ancient writers and grouping them under moral headings; his choice of Latin authors, however, would have been unthinkable a generation before.

15

But the real successor to Lovato was the Paduan notary Albertino Mussato (1262–1329). He had exchanged Latin verse with Lovato and shared with him a passion for the tragedies of Seneca. Not only was he the author of a Latin dialogue explaining Seneca's metric schemes more fully but he also provided Latin summaries of the plays and even wrote a Senecan tragedy himself. Mussato was also a pioneer historian. In his *Historiae* he modelled his narrative not on the annalistic tradition of the Middle Ages but on the style of Livy, Caesar, and Sallust. What proved, however, to be Mussato's greatest achievement as a humanist was his revival of classical tragedy.

In 1314 Padua was seriously threatened. Cangrande della Scala, the ambitious Lord of Verona, may have been one of Dante's heroes, but it was plain that his intention was to conquer all the neighbouring city states. After Vicenza had been swallowed, Padua was clearly his next victim. To arouse the Paduans to the seriousness of their danger was, accordingly, imperative. Mussato therefore decided to write a tragedy in Latin verse, the *Ecerinis*, in which he dramatized the rise and progress of the appalling tyranny of Ezzelino III da Romano. The lesson was clear to the Paduans, and as a piece of political propaganda the *Ecerinis* could scarcely have proved more successful. What interests us here is that it was the first tragedy written since classical times in classical metres. As a literary drama, the *Ecerinis* proved successful throughout Italy, being read and commented upon just as if it were the work of an ancient classical writer.

One of the results of the *Ecerinis* is also not without interest. No crowning of a poet with laurel had been recorded since the days of the Emperor Domitian in the first century A.D. But now the grateful Paduans decided to revive this honour and to bestow it upon Mussato, a clear indication of how far the town had been conditioned by humanist influence in a single generation. Mussato's crowning in 1315 was a local ceremony. But news of it ran through Italy and

16

stimulated Dante's longing for a similar honour. Later Petrarch saw to it that he also received his laurels, in his case in the Capitol.

With Mussato, humanism had firmly established itself in Padua. Nor were some of the neighbouring towns slow in developing a humanism of their own. Exchanges with Mussato and his friends carried the seed to nearby Vicenza. Here the notary Benvenuto Campesani (1255–1323) exchanged friendly Latin verse with the Paduan scholars, and eventually addressed Latin invectives against them when Padua ranged itself against Cangrande della Scala. The reappearance in about 1300 of the long-lost poems of Catullus was hailed by Campesani with a Latin epigram. But his greatest achievement proved to be his influence on Ferreto Ferreti (1297–1337), who besides showing himself a competent Latin poet also produced a history of Italy in Latin, which reveals him as the foremost Italian historian of his time.

Another place in which the influence of Mussato was strongly felt was Venice, where chancery officials and local schoolmasters exchanged with him Latin verse dealing with political matters. These exchanges were actually 'inspired' by the Venetian government; in fact, throughout the fourteenth century Venetian humanism in general retained a political bias, not surprising in view of the isolation of the Republic and of its policy.

None the less, there were strong similarities between the humanism of Padua and that of Vicenza and Venice. To find a different brand of humanism we must turn instead to Verona, the town which under Cangrande della Scala had become one of the great political powers in north Italy. After the fall of the Roman Empire in the West in A.D. 476 Verona had become joint capital with Ravenna of the Gothic kingdom of Italy, and throughout the so-called 'dark ages' it had retained its prominence. Among the legacies of its ancient magnificence, which Cangrande was doing much to revive, there was the Chapter Library founded in the ninth century by the Archdeacon Pacificus—and still open today. The riches of this library included many manuscripts of the Latin classics, several of which were as early as the fifth and sixth centuries A.D. This wealth, untouched for a very long time, began to be noticed again during the later years of the Duecento. What further stimulated this interest was the arrival from France about 1300 of a text of Catullus, the greatest Veronese poet, whose work had remained unknown and unread since Bishop Ratherius's study of it in the tenth century. The rediscovery of Catullus in Verona led to exchanges with the humanists of Padua and Vicenza. But the earliest humanists of Verona developed on wholly different lines. Their classical pursuits did not manifest themselves in Latin poetry, or the description of contemporary events in elegant Latin prose, but in sterner works of scholarship.

Giovanni de Matociis (fl. 1306–20), the 'mansionarius' of Verona Cathedral, used his wide knowledge of the Latin classics in the compilation, sometime between 1306 and 1320, of a *Historia Imperialis* stretching from Augustus to Charlemagne. He also composed a tract on the Elder and the Younger Pliny. During the Middle Ages these two writers had been believed to be one person. But Giovanni had under his eyes the letters of the Younger Pliny, a work then unknown in Italy outside the Verona Chapter Library, and with the additional help of the life of the Elder Pliny by Suetonius, he was able to prove beyond doubt the separate identities of the authors of the Natural History and the Letters.

The tract on the two Plinys, rather than the bulky *Historia Imperialis*, was the supreme achievement of early Veronese humanism, since it showed for the first time the critical use of classical sources in establishing an important point in literary history. But for the moment it was an isolated achievement. Benzo d'Alessandria, the scholar who anticipated Petrarch in more than one way, settled in Verona only during the third decade of the century; while Guglielmo da Pastrengo, whose *De Viris Illustribus* again relies on the resources of the Chapter Library, really belongs to the age of Petrarch—that is to say, when humanism was already beyond its primitive stage.

Benzo d'Alessandria, who was Cangrande della Scala's chancellor for several years, naturally knew the Chapter Library well. But before settling in Verona he had travelled extensively through north and central Italy, and what he saw during his journeys—and he kept his eyes open—he also incorporated in his huge chronicle. The exceptional length of the text has, not surprisingly, prevented its complete publication so far, but a few sections have appeared. It is certainly a notable piece of work, using classical texts and antiquarian materials, such as inscriptions, ancient remains, etc., in a way without parallel before Petrarch.

Verona had thus made its mark in the humanist field by the end of the first quarter of the fourteenth century. Yet the age of this early humanism was also the age of Dante (1265–1321), who remained to the end quite aloof from it. Despite his poetic stature, despite his insight into Virgil's writings, which revealed the mind of that author with a clarity unrivalled until then, his actual knowledge of the classics was not much wider than that of the average master of grammar. There is, for instance, no evidence that he read in the Chapter Library during his visits to Verona. Rather than heralding the Renaissance, Dante marks the end of the Middle Ages. His Latin and his rhetoric remained those of the tradition in which he had been brought up. His *Monarchia* and *De Vulgari Eloquentia* were the works of a scholar of genius, but none the less medieval to the core, while his Latin eclogues modelled on Virgil had had predecessors during the twelfth century. In short, though an exile from Florence from 1302 until his death in 1321, Dante remained to the end a typical exponent of Florentine rather than Italian culture in general.

In Florence, and equally in Bologna, one might search in vain for any real departure from medieval tradition until the second half of the fourteenth century. Not so in Naples, where some humanist activity was already flourishing before Boccaccio settled there (about 1328) or Petrarch visited the town. Humanism here, however, was not the same as in north Italy. Whereas in the north it arose from the enthusiasm and dedication of a few individuals, in the south it was a courtly humanism fostered by the King's patronage.

Naples was the capital of the only monarchy in Italy. Its domain extended to the southern tip of the peninsula and had included Sicily also until 1282, when the island passed under the rule of the Kings of Aragon. As a centralized monarchy, the Neapolitan kingdom had avoided the party conflict between Guelfs and Ghibellines. Instead, it was subject to endemic baronial rebellions of a kind impossible elsewhere in Italy. After the defeat and death of its last Hohenstaufen ruler, Manfredi, at the battle of Benevento in 1266, the kingdom came under a French dynasty, the Angevins, who brought with them a harsh tyranny and a taste for theology. The first two Angevin rulers, Charles I and his son Charles II, showed no particular enthusiasm for literature. But with Robert I (1309–1343) the situation altered, since the new king was an intellectual with a taste for theological disputation and the preaching of sermons. His own scholarship was not outstanding, and his Latin was pedestrian by humanist standards, but his devotion to learning cannot be doubted. The advancement of medicine was among his aims. It was because of this, and also because he wished to broaden his theological notions, that he employed in the royal library scholars from the Greek-speaking parts of the Italian south, to translate into Latin various treatises by Galen and Hippocrates and the works of Greek divines. It was indeed characteristic of Robert that he should have been the man to secure the crowning of Petrarch with the poetic laurels in 1341.

This is a significant example of the way in which early Italian humanism provided a foundation in some important respects for the Renaissance. Yet though none can deny that it contributed towards the achievement of Petrarch, this great humanist was also as much the cultural child of the papal court at Avignon.

Pope Benedict XI, the meek successor of the formidable Boniface VIII, died in 1304, and the newly elected pope, Clement V, who up to that time had been Archbishop of Bordeaux, decided to reside in Provence. Eventually the Papacy settled in Avignon and remained there until 1377, when Gregory XI finally brought it back to Rome. As the seat of the Papacy, Avignon became the effective centre of Christendom, though Rome never ceased to be its spiritual capital and the goal of countless pilgrims. It is, therefore, not surprising to find during the first quarter of the century some humanists in Avignon. We hear, for instance, of a Provençal clerk called Raymond Subirani (who had been for some time in the service of our Edward II) enthusiastically collecting manuscripts of ancient Latin writers. The same was being done by Landolfo Colonna, a Roman noble and canon of Chartres, who secured, among other things, a transcript of the now lost fifth-century Livy, then preserved in the library of Chartres Cathedral. Landolfo Colonna also played a leading role in the transmission of other important classical texts, and both he and Subirani prepared the ground for the young Petrarch.

Meanwhile, in painting and sculpture, Nicola and Giovanni Pisano were seeking their inspiration direct from classical sculpture, as indeed some sculptors in south Italy had also done in the time of Frederick II; with Giotto, painting finally abandoned the Byzantine tradition, turning from two-dimensional abstract art to a three-dimensional imitation of nature. The Gothic style never became acclimatized in Italy, so that in art the progression to Renaissance ideals was really from the Romanesque and Byzantine.

We may notice, in passing, the absence of any Italian vernacular literature until the second quarter of the thirteenth century. What was written before then in the everyday tongue hardly deserved to be called literature at all. Here the delaying factor was the closeness of Italian dialects to Latin. Men considered the latter the only language fit for literary purposes. Hence when Italian courtly poetry developed about 1220 at the Sicilian court of the Emperor Frederick II (1194–1250) it was forced to rely on models from medieval Provence. But since the distance between the poems of Frederick's courtiers and modern Italian poetry is less, technically and linguistically, than that separating Chaucer from English verse today, one can see how Italian poetry was able to achieve in less than one century its supreme masterpiece with Dante. In the first Italian prose, also, medieval influence never went very deep, and here too Dante was the first to show what it could really achieve.

Italian literature by-passed the medieval phase because of the lay character of Italian culture. As in early humanism, early vernacular literature in Italy was mostly the work of laymen and not clerics. In other words, those concerned did not subordinate their existence in this world to their expectations in the next. But it is idle to speculate on what is an extremely complex problem and one to which no solution can be offered. None the less, if we scrutinize the origins of the Italian Renaissance we shall be driven to conclude that this unique event was the result of unique influences. The change from the free town to the principality was crucial, since, once humanism had reached a certain stage, patronage became essential to its further development and the new Italian rulers were not slow in providing this patronage.

# 2

# Petrarch and Boccaccio

DANTE created the Italian language, Petrarch and Boccaccio created Italian literature. Like Shakespeare, Dante found admirers but no immediate imitators; or, perhaps, one might say more accurately, the imitations of the *Divine Comedy* written during the fourteenth and fifteenth centuries were of such poor quality that we can hardly call them 'literature'. On the other hand, Petrarch dominated the European lyric, just as European story-telling would have found it difficult to develop without Boccaccio. What is more, Petrarch and Boccaccio were chiefly responsible for the consolidation of humanism. Until the sixteenth century Petrarch and Boccaccio were mainly, though not exclusively, known outside Italy as the authors of Latin treatises on moral philosophy, mythology, and geography; even in their own Italy their reputation as humanists was certainly not inferior to their reputation as writers in the spoken tongue.

As a humanist, Petrarch (1304–1374) belonged to quite a different class from Boccaccio, who always considered himself Petrarch's disciple. Petrarch's strength lay in the fact that besides being equipped with a formidable genius he brought together the achievements of the humanist groups before him. The son of one of Dante's fellow exiles, Petrarch was influenced little by the mediocre Convenevole da Prato or the professors of civil law of the University of Bologna, where he wasted three years and secured no degree; he learned chiefly from the Papal Curia at Avignon and from his own father, ser Petracco. Though he was a prosperous

23

lawyer, Petrarch's father had a taste for classical writings, and was careful to encourage the same taste in his son. At Avignon the young man received further encouragement from Raymond Subirani and Landolfo Colonna. Colonna's copy of Livy aroused his particular enthusiasm and may well have started him on his career as a textual critic of ancient Latin authors.

His passion for classical antiquity manifested itself in several ways. There was his ambition to assert himself as a new Virgil, a new Cicero, and a new Livy. There was his ambition to revive the ideals of classical antiquity as far as this was possible in a Christian world. There was his intense anxiety to rescue as much as he could of the literature of the Roman world, which involved him in an intensive search for manuscripts. Now the discovery of a manuscript in some forgotten corner of a cathedral or monastic library immediately presented a moral problem. Very few private persons owned books then, and even fewer possessed copies of ancient authors. Thus the discoverer was faced with two alternatives: either to steal it or copy it. Some humanists are known to have chosen the former method. Petrarch chose the latter. When in 1333 he discovered Cicero's oration *Pro Archia* in Liège he copied it from beginning to end, and most of the known manuscripts of the text descend directly or indirectly from Petrarch's transcript. The same happened again in 1345 when he unearthed in Verona Cicero's letters *Ad Atticum*.

As the years passed, through copying, purchase, and gifts, Petrarch succeeded in assembling the greatest collection of Latin classics in private hands of his time, a collection which no monastic or chapter library, not even the Papal Library, could rival either in quantity or variety. Collecting manuscripts was, however, not enough for Petrarch. He sedulously studied the text, compared it with that of other manuscripts, introduced emendations, and penned explanatory notes in the margin. In fact, he virtually prepared critical editions of some of the works of Cicero, Livy, and St.

Augustine, scarcely inferior to those produced when humanism had reached its zenith. Moreover, his study of these authors was not just a matter of textual criticism divorced from interest in their subject-matter. He attempted to derive as much as he could from them—and not merely to enrich his store of knowledge. For him, antiquity alone presented a unique way of life which had been forgotten and which he believed it was imperative to regain. It meant a return to Rome's departed glory through the practise of the virtues which had made the Romans great. The revolution of Cola di Rienzo, the Roman notary, who tried in 1347 to revive the Roman Republic and proclaimed himself tribune of Rome, persuaded Petrarch for a moment that his wildest hopes were being realized. But to govern fourteenth-century Rome according to the precepts of Livy was not practical politics, and Cola's rule collapsed after a few months and with it also Petrarch's political hopes. But his craving for fame never abandoned him. He realized that his goals were incompatible with those of medieval Christianity. Yet despite much searching of his conscience and periodic escapes into solitude, despite the plain message in the writings of his beloved St. Augustine, the attainment of glory remained his greatest desire.

Could he attain his desire? Of this he had no doubt, and he saw literary achievement as the path to it. When still in his thirties he had mapped out his literary career and had realized that the kind of glory he was seeking could be achieved only by one who wrote in Latin. Accordingly, he planned two major works, one in poetry and the other in prose. The *Aeneid* was the supreme Latin epic, Livy the greatest of Roman historians. He proposed to emulate these by writing a poem on the Punic Wars, the *Affrica*, and a prose account of the lives of famous men from remotest times, the *De Viris Illustribus*. It was chiefly for the *Affrica*, even though it was still far from complete, that Petrarch received his poetic laurels in 1341. Yet when he died in 1374 neither of these works had been released by their fastidious

25

author. Petrarch wrote many other works in Latin. In verse, besides three books of metric epistles modelled on Horace, he wrote a Latin comedy, now lost (the *Philologia Philostrati*), some eclogues, in which he sought to emulate Virgil's *Bucolics*, and some minor poems and epigrams. His prose works include the *Secretum*, an imaginary dialogue in which he laid bare his own spiritual conflicts; some treatises in praise of the monastic life which he himself had been so careful to avoid, and of the solitary life in which he so often indulged; and a bulky moral treatise, inspired mainly by Seneca, the *De remediis utriusque fortunae*, in which he employed his classical learning to support a typically medieval outlook. He composed a handbook for travellers from Genoa to Jerusalem, though he himself had never embarked on such a journey. Petrarch's greatest achievements in prose, however, were the *Ad Familiares* in twenty-four books and the *Seniles* in eighteen. In these he revealed to his correspondents his aspirations, his hopes, and his disappointments, appearing now as adviser, now as confidant, now as teacher, and providing a mass of invaluable autobiographical material.

In the epistles he was both consciously following the example of Cicero and Seneca and to some extent presenting himself in the garb of a classical writer. In fact, the last book of the *Ad Familiares* is made up of letters addressed to the greatest writers of antiquity, such as Homer, Virgil, Livy, Cicero and Seneca. They are treated as equals and even criticized now and then; in his letter to Cicero, for instance, he does not hide his disapproval of some of his political actions. Here, more than in any other work, Petrarch tried to think and express himself like an ancient and yet revealed himself as a man of his time, with only the trappings and not the spirit of antiquity. His Latin style is certainly closer to classical models than that of any humanist who preceded or immediately succeeded him, but his outlook has all the fears, limitations, and prejudices of the later Middle Ages.

In politics he may have yearned for the Roman Republic,

advocated a revival of the ancient city of Rome, and deplored the evils which haunted the Italy of his day. But in practice he was glad to accept the patronage of some of the Italian rulers who in fact fostered the very evils against which he was so ready to inveigh. Between republican Florence and tyrant-ridden Milan he had no hesitation in choosing Milan as his residence for some years, and why? He knew very well that life would be more comfortable in the shadow of a princely court than in a free town.

Petrarch's humanism was entirely Latin. In his time, those who knew Greek in Italy—the Greek-speaking territories in the south and Sicily excepted—were very few indeed and their scholarly activities quite insignificant. Petrarch made an attempt to learn Greek, but his efforts were never more than half-hearted. Admittedly, after he had been taught for some weeks in 1342 by the Byzantine monk, Barlaam, the lessons came to an abrupt end owing to his teacher's elevation to a bishopric. Yet he would not have found it impossible to find another teacher of Greek in cosmopolitan Avignon. If his knowledge of the language hardly went beyond the elements this must be attributed to his unwillingness to continue learning it. In spite of this he was the father of Renaissance Greek studies. Not only was he the first Italian humanist to own Greek manuscripts but he was also instrumental in inducing the Greek-speaking Italian, Leontius Pilatus, whom he met in Padua, to go to Florence with Boccaccio and turn the Homeric poems into Latin for him.

Petrarch's exceptional gifts as a humanist were quickly noticed by his contemporaries and he won a host of friends on both sides of the Alps. In Avignon he met many foreigners like Richard de Bury, the bibliophile Bishop of Durham, from whom he hoped to gain information about the exact location of the 'Ultima Thule' of the ancients. Through all these contacts, he was able to exert a powerful influence upon the development of humanism. Nor was this all. His own Latin writings were approached by his friends with the awe usually accorded to classical authors, so much so that they endeavoured to model themselves and their writings on him.

Despite his immense humanist achievement, however, Petrarch is now mainly remembered for his vernacular love poems in praise of Laura. Throughout his life he affected to despise his writings in Italian but never ceased working on them. His *Trionfi*, a series of visions showing the triumphal processions of Love, Chastity, Death, Fame, Time, and Eternity—a typically medieval conception but tempered by a humanist outlook—were actually meant to compete with Dante, whose fame Petrarch ignored publicly but secretly envied. During the fifteenth century the *Trionfi* enjoyed a high success in Italy second only to that of the *Divine Comedy*; yet their rhythmic beauty and occasionally sparkling imagery hardly relieve the dreariness of the subject-matter. They certainly do not show Petrarch at his best. His undoubted masterpiece was the love lyrics of the *Canzoniere*, where he expressed his unrequited passion for Laura in poetry which united sincere and deep feeling with an extraordinarily beautiful diction.

When Italian lyric poetry came into existence during the first half of the thirteenth century it took over many of the conventions of the Provençal love lyric. For instance, poets were permitted to celebrate in their verse only a lady who fulfilled two conditions. She must not return the poet's love and must be already married to somebody else. As time went on, the poet's lady became more and more abstract, more a personification of every kind of perfection than a real human being.

Such was Dante's Beatrice, and in his *Vita Nuova* Dante wrote what one critic has rightly called a *Legenda Sanctae Beatricis*. With Cino da Pistoia (c. 1265–1337), with whom Dante exchanged verse, the Italian love lyric saw a new development. The poet's lady now began to regain some human features, and the ecstasy or despair of the poet was replaced by an elegiac emotion suffused with gentle melancholy. This new element makes Cino's verses a bridge linking the lyrics of Dante with those of Petrarch.

In his *Canzoniere* Petrarch conformed with tradition by sighing for a married woman. Who Laura was, or even whether she really existed, does not concern us. What really matters is that she is alive in Petrarch's poetry. He displays an uncanny ability to describe his feelings exactly in lyric terms, and a rare capacity for psychological self-analysis. When we consider that these qualities were matched by an exquisite sense of rhythm, a sparkling range of imagery, and a use of conceits seldom degenerating into hyperbole, as well as by an effortless balance of form and matter, which brings home to the reader the subtlest shades of the poet's appreciation of the beauty of the physical world; when we realize that all this was achieved with immediacy and spontaneity, and with a simplicity not to be found outside the ancient classics, it is scarcely surprising that Petrarch's *Canzoniere* proved at once an immense success. More than this, it was a kind of poetry which was superficially quite easy to imitate; and the apparent ease with which one could echo Petrarch's sighs was partly responsible for what we now call Petrarchism.

Though Petrarch was undoubtedly the greatest of all humanist teachers, with pupils all over Western Europe, he never held a university chair and never taught. Among those who felt the attraction of his spell, one of the first, if not the very first, was Boccaccio. He could scarcely have been more different from his master, not only in temperament but also in outlook and in his approach to scholarship. He wrote both in Latin and Italian, and like him he was at first more famous as a Latin than as an Italian author, though nowadays his Latin writings are little read.

Boccaccio (1313–1375), too, was a Florentine, though he was an expatriate during part of his youth. His reputed birth in Paris is as much a fairy-tale as the identification of Fiammetta, the heroine of his autobiographical romance, with a Maria d'Aquino (who unfortunately never existed).

Part of his youth was spent in the Naples which he described so strikingly in the *Decameron* story of Andreuccio da Perugia; and here he divided his time between his mercantile duties and the pursuit of letters. His earlier literary efforts are in conformity with medieval tradition and reveal a taste for the conventional rhetoric of his time. Also typically medieval was his early predilection for Ovid, while Paolo da Perugia, a teacher of grammar, stimulated in him an interest in ancient mythology which endured for the rest of his life.

Boccaccio's first glimpse of Petrarch was when, as one of the crowd of spectators, he saw him in Naples in 1341 being publicly examined by King Robert I before his crowning with laurel. Later, however, he got to know him personally and visited him more than once in north Italy. The resulting influence was overwhelming and he eagerly collected the writings of the older man and strove to imitate him. He, too, tried his hand at Latin eclogues and set about collecting as many classical texts as he could. In this he was seriously handicapped by lack of means and influence. Nevertheless, he was able to profit from the discoveries of ancient texts made at Montecassino by Zanobi da Strada, which included Tacitus and much of what was then unknown of Apuleius. He was also the first to read some forgotten orations of Cicero and these he naturally communicated to Petrarch.

Boccaccio compiled several massive treatises in Latin which were still being found valuable during the high Renaissance. His *De Montibus* was much sought after as an encyclopaedia of classical geography; and his disciple, Domenico Silvestri, paid it the compliment of following it with the *De Insulis*. But the Latin works which most contributed to Boccaccio's fame were his *De Casibus virorum illustrium* (which furnished a source for Chaucer's *Monk's Tale*) and the *De Genealogia Deorum*, where he gave an account of all the gods and demigods of the pagan Pantheon. These works show quite clearly that Boccaccio viewed scholarship mainly from an encyclopaedist's angle. Moreover, his temperament had not the patience and resolution which are essential to accurate scholarship. Yet by his very difference he filled the gaps which existed in the humanist activities of Petrarch. What is more, he did for Greek studies something of what Petrarch might have done.

There is no evidence that Boccaccio had any dealings with the Greek translators employed by King Robert I during his years in Naples. His extant commonplace books disclose, none the less, that he already had an interest in Greek at an early stage in his career. It was, however, only when Leontius Pilatus came to stay with him in Florence in 1360 that his Greek studies really started. In taking Pilatus into his home, Boccaccio showed himself readier than Petrarch to make sacrifices for the cause of Greek learning. Furthermore, he succeeded in obtaining a lectureship for Pilatus in the University of Florence—the first teaching post in Greek, it may be noted, in a Western European university. Admittedly, Pilatus attracted only a few students and none of them succeeded in forming a tradition of Greek studies in Florence. On the other hand, his Latin versions of the *Iliad* and *Odyssey*, though hardly satisfactory as translations, remained unrivalled and in circulation until the middle of the fifteenth century.

Boccaccio's greatest enthusiasm was one which Petrarch failed entirely to share with him. He felt something near to veneration for Dante, whom he saw as the very incarnation of poetry. He looked to him in the same way as Petrarch looked to the great classical writers and wrote a biography of him in Italian which is an unfortunate blend of fact and fiction. On Dante's *Inferno* he lectured publicly in Florence during the last years of his life.

As a humanist, Boccaccio differed considerably from Petrarch, despite his close and frequent exchanges with him. He was no textual critic and the patient collation of manuscripts was clearly distasteful to him. What attracted him most in the ancient writers was what they had to tell him about history, geography, and mythology—in short, the factual information available in their works. None the less, he was also able to appreciate their writings as masterpieces of prose or poetry. Poetry remained to the very end his ruling passion and his self-made epitaph ended 'Studium fuit alma poesis'. This above all was at the root of his worship of Dante. It was characteristic of him, in the last sections of his treatise on mythology, to rise to the defence of poetry against the theologians who were attacking it. His enthusiasm for Greek was livelier than Petrarch's and so was his attachment to the medieval rhetorical tradition. This is not surprising in view of his early life in Angevin Naples. Yet what turned Boccaccio into a humanist was not so much the Naples of King Robert I, nor the Florence of the generation after Dante; it was Petrarch, for he widened Boccaccio's intellectual horizons and communicated to him his enthusiasm for ancient literature.

Today Boccaccio is remembered only for his vernacular works and principally for the *Decameron*. To Italian prose, the *Decameron* is what Petrarch's *Canzoniere* is to Italian poetry. And yet the parallel is not as accurate as it might seem. After the *Divine Comedy* no poetry written in Italy— not even the *Canzoniere*—ever approached its supreme standards. Dante's prose, on the other hand, never reached the same dazzling heights. Both the *Convivio* and the *Vita Nuova* were conventional works, one following the tradition of the troubadours, the other striving to express in a modern language the Latin reasoning of the schools of theology and philosophy. In contrast, Boccaccio's prose possessed a vitality and freedom never achieved by Dante. The earlier work of Boccaccio, it is true, is medieval in outlook and subject-matter and does not foreshadow the *Decameron* any more than Dante's *Convivio* foreshadowed the *Divine Comedy*. But in the *Decameron* Boccaccio's genius found a chance of expressing all that was in him, of achieving the comic and the pathetic, the grave and the satirical, the heroic and the vile—in short, of reproducing with a new degree of fidelity the world in which he moved.

Boccaccio drew the subject-matter of his tales from a multitude of sources. These included some of Eastern origin, old pious legends, the Latin classics, the French 'Fabliaux', and earlier collections of short stories in Italian. As in the *Arabian Nights*, the hundred stories were placed within a 'frame' and imagined as having been told during the space of ten days in 1348 by seven young women and three young men, who had sought refuge from the ravages of the Black Death in a country house near Florence.

The stories deal with extraordinary adventures, examples of magnanimity, practical jokes, clever deceptions, and so on. Their scene is very often Florence, or at any rate Tuscany, though not invariably so. As for the heroes and heroines, they are drawn from every class of society, from kings down to peasants. But whatever their nationality or station, whether real or fictitious, they invariably bear a striking resemblance to the Florentines of Boccaccio's time in their outlook, tastes, and prejudices.

In the field of the 'novella' Boccaccio's *Decameron* opened new horizons and established new standards. Now for the first time short stories achieved a genuine fullness and dramatic quality. Often imitated, the *Decameron* was never seriously threatened in its supremacy as a portrayal of the human scene as it was just when medieval civilization was moving towards its end. In fact, European story-telling down to the end of the Renaissance and even afterwards owed more to the *Decameron* than to any other single work.

The debt of Renaissance literature and humanism to Petrarch and Boccaccio was considerable indeed. Humanism dominated the intellectual life of Italy for about a century and a half after their day, and its mark may still be perceived in education today. Thanks mainly to Petrarch, the rules and conventions of medieval rhetoric, with its clichés and its emphasis upon the rhythmic stressing of clauses, went out of fashion, to be replaced by Ciceronianism. But he achieved even more through the influence he exerted upon his many friends, an influence noticeable even during his lifetime in almost every important princely and city chancery in Italy. The search for copies of the ancient classics was stimulated, if not really initiated, by him; the revival of the classical technique of letter-writing, the textual study of Roman writers, which has occupied so many scholars since the second half of the fourteenth century, were further results of his influence.

Geographically, the influence of Boccaccio proved very much more limited. Petrarch influenced the whole of Italy. Boccaccio influenced Florence. His circle of friends were the direct ancestors of Florentine fifteenth-century humanism. Theirs was a humanism neither as comprehensive nor as deep as Petrarch's. Yet it was instrumental in liberating classical mythology from much of the nonsense which had accumulated during the Middle Ages. It was a humanism with a bent towards mythology and geography, one which conceived history as a series of biographies and anecdotes. Its greatest achievement was the introduction of Greek studies into Florence. It is true that these studies were short-lived and left no tradition. None the less, they bequeathed an awareness of the great significance of Greek. Had it not been for these earlier efforts it would have been less possible for Greek studies to start again in Florence in 1397—and this time they were not to be interrupted. Behind the Byzantine Emanuel Chrysoloras, who taught in Florence from 1397 to 1400, lurks the spirit of Boccaccio.

# 3

# The rediscovery of the ancient world

THE deaths of Petrarch in 1374 and Boccaccio in 1375 were seen by their contemporaries as the demise of poetry itself. In this they were not altogether wrong, for no verse of real merit was written again in Italy until the second half of the fifteenth century. The foundations of humanism, however, did not crumble away with their deaths. By then the tradition was flourishing from Venice down to Naples. Neither Petrarch nor Boccaccio had ever taught formally, but with the two Giovannis of Ravenna (Giovanni Malpaghini and Giovanni Conversini) the schools found room for humanist teaching, while humanist rhetoric was clearly behind the practice of all the great Italian chanceries. Humanist learning became an essential qualification for employment as chancellor or secretary to prince or republic, and proved a valuable asset in the actual service of the state. During the tremendous struggle between Florence and the ruler of Milan, Giangaleazzo Visconti, the usual forms of warfare were accompanied by a violent 'paper war' in which each side vituperated against the other in choice Latin. The main contestants were two distinguished humanists, Antonio Loschi, then Chancellor of the Duke of Milan, and Coluccio Salutati, Chancellor of the Florentine Republic.

Though scarcely a man of first-rate ability, Salutati (1331–1406) was a significant figure in the development of humanism in the generation after Petrarch. He was heir to the humanism of Petrarch and Boccaccio, and instrumental in transmitting their legacy to successive generations.

35

Boccaccio's fame as a humanist—and this is by no means an attempt to diminish his achievement—has perhaps been unduly magnified by his greatness as a prose-writer. There is no doubt that, purely as a humanist, Salutati is more important than Boccaccio. That his Latin writings display little literary merit is true, but he had amassed an imposing library of which about one hundred volumes are still extant, and which included several classical texts rescued by him from oblivion. What is more, he was the patron, stimulator, and adviser of every great figure in Florentine humanism of the next generation. Again, it was he alone who was responsible for the starting of Greek studies on humanist lines more than thirty years after Leontius Pilatus had relinquished his Florentine lectureship.

Salutati was, in short, the dictator of the humanist world of Italy from 1374 until his death in 1406. Though he had never met Petrarch and exchanged but few letters with him, his ambition was to be a second Petrarch. Certainly, if there was one person who consolidated the links between humanism and politics initiated by Petrarch it was Salutati. Boccaccio's influence upon him was more intense; the *De Genealogia Deorum* affected him deeply, and his great love of poetry and his defence of it against the theologians also originated in part from Boccaccio.

Salutati moulded the generation of humanists which succeeded him. In fact, he was chiefly responsible for the rise of such outstanding figures as Poggio Bracciolini (1380–1459) and Leonardo Bruni (1374–1444). He stimulated in them a passion—'passion' is the right word here—for searching out the texts of Latin writers which had not been seen since the ninth or tenth century. During the first half of the fifteenth century this search was perhaps the most important humanist activity. Salutati himself had set an exceptional example by making Propertius, Tibullus, and Cicero's *Ad Familiares* available again. Unfortunately, during the early years of the fifteenth century both Poggio and Bruni left Florence, where prospects appeared not too encouraging, and secured appointments in the Papal Chancery. Here they were soon joined by other humanists. Little wonder, then, that Florentine humanist supremacy did not survive the death of Salutati. By the year 1420 the most prominent humanist centre in Italy was no longer Florence but the Papal Court.

The great schism which had torn the Church asunder since the election of Urban VI in 1378 was eventually ended by the Council of Constance (1414–17) and by the election of Pope Martin V in 1417. As far as the discovery of classical texts was concerned, this council proved exceptionally important. When in 1414 the whole Papal Court resorted to Constance, the humanists in its chancery included, it was quickly realized that the neighbouring monasteries owned particularly wealthy libraries. The humanists were not slow in dedicating their spare time to the hunting of ancient texts, and an expedition by Poggio, which took him as far as Cluny in France, yielded two unknown orations of Cicero, while his first visit to St. Gall enabled him to find the poem of Valerius Flaccus on the Argonauts, the commentary on some of Cicero's speeches by Asconius Pedianus, and a complete text of the *Institutions* of Quintilian, hitherto available only in part. A year later, in 1417, he once more inspected the St. Gall library. This time the yield was even richer and included Manilius's *Astronomicon*, the *Punica* of Silius Italicus, the *De Rerum Natura* of Lucretius, and the history of Ammianus Marcellinus. A journey to France and Germany later during the same year was rewarded with the discovery of no less than eight new speeches of Cicero as well as the *Sylvae* of Statius.

Compared with those of Poggio, all the other discoveries of ancient texts made during the fifteenth century appear insignificant. In 1494 Giorgio Galbiate found a considerable group of unknown classical writings at Bobbio, but these were almost entirely grammatical or rhetorical treatises and included no works by major writers. In fact, after Poggio the only discovery of real importance was that of the minor works of Tacitus made by Enoch of Ascoli at Fulda about 1455. More Tacitus and also some Livy were found later during the sixteenth century when the age of the great discoveries was virtually over.

The importance of Poggio lies principally in those finds of his which restored to us many of the masterpieces of Latin literature. That of Leonardo Bruni, on the other hand, lies mainly in the field of Greek studies, and about these studies two misconceptions must be cleared up. The first is the prevalent view that during the Middle Ages Greek was quite unknown in Western Europe. The second, which still has some adherents, is that the knowledge of Greek was re-introduced into the West by refugee scholars after the Turkish conquest of Constantinople in 1453. As far as the first misconception is concerned, it is true that during the Middle Ages the number of people in Western Europe who knew Greek was exceedingly small. On the other hand, there was no period between the sixth and the fifteenth centuries when there were none at all. In France the writings of the pseudo-Dionysius were turned into Latin during the ninth and again during the twelfth century. Some writings of Plato and Aristotle were latinized in Sicily during the second half of the twelfth century, and practically the whole of Aristotle as well as much else during the late twelfth and thirteenth centuries. Then, as we have already seen, many of the treatises of Galen were translated at Naples during the first half of the fourteenth century. As for the belief that knowledge of Greek was secured in the West only after the Turkish conquest of Constantinople in 1453, when many Byzantine scholars fled westwards, this cannot be taken seriously any longer.

In the field of humanist Greek studies Leontius Pilatus, who turned all Homer and some Euripides into Latin, was something of a pioneer; not only because he was the first to teach Greek formally in a Western university but also because (though many translators from the Greek had preceded him in the West) he was the first one to translate

purely lite... tradition of
Greek st... pils made a
name for... ntly, not long
after his... more without
Greek. ... wever, died out
altoget... reek was taught
again i... the century. Also
thank... lecided in 1396 to
estab... re, invited Emanuel
Chry... Byzantine scholars of
the time, ... rysoloras started his
Florentine cours... emic Greek studies in
the West. By then Salutati ... old to start learning a
new language. But the younger members of his circle eagerly
flocked to Chrysoloras's lecture room, while the wealthiest
of them, Palla Strozzi, saw to it that Greek studies did not
suffer through lack of essential texts. Pier Paolo Vergerio,
Jacopo Angeli and Leonardo Bruni were among those who
went to sit at the feet of Chrysoloras. Among them, Bruni
was certainly the greatest: his translations already show not
only the technique but also all the other features which distinguish Renaissance translating from that of the preceding
centuries.

Medieval translators rendered the Greek text word by
word. What mattered to them was the letter of the work and
nothing else. But Chrysoloras told his pupils again and again
that to the translator the spirit and real meaning of the text
mattered much more. Little wonder, then, that such an
approach was readily taken over by Bruni in his translations,
but first of all an adequate supply of texts was essential.
During the fifteenth century the search for manuscripts of
ancient Latin writers had as its counterpart a search just as
intensive and dramatic for the works of Greek classical
authors. Already as early as 1395 Jacopo Angeli had sailed
to Constantinople and returned home with several Greek
books when he brought Chrysoloras over in 1397. On
Chrysoloras's return to the East in 1403 he was followed by

Guarino da Verona, who collected a considerable number of Greek volumes and brought them back to Italy in 1408. The same was done by Francesco Filelfo, who was in the Byzantine capital from 1421 to 1427, and by the Florentine priest Christoforo Buondelmonti, who was in Greece from 1414 until 1430. Special journeys were also made to Greek lands in order to secure manuscripts. Aurispa, who travelled in the Byzantine domains from 1405 to 1413 and again during 1421–3, practically became a dealer in Greek manuscripts; and similar journeys, though prompted by a less commercial outlook, were made by Ciriaco of Ancona, who is chiefly remembered today as the father of Greek archaeology. In these ways very substantial collections of Greek manuscripts were formed in Italy during the first half of the fifteenth century. In Florence the chief collectors were Palla Strozzi, Antonio Corbinelli, Giannozzo Manetti and, above all, Niccolò Niccoli, whose library remained unsurpassed in his lifetime; in Venice, Francesco Barbaro was the chief collector.

During the second half of the fifteenth century the libraries of princes became the main repositories of Greek texts. Pope Nicholas V (1447–55) saw to the enrichment of the Vatican Library, while Federigo, Duke of Urbino (1422–1482), did the same for his own library. Again, the Medici, particularly Lorenzo the Magnificent (1449–1492), built up an exceptional collection of Greek volumes. The greatest fifteenth-century collector of such books, however, was the Greek-born Cardinal Bessarion (1403–1472); he presented his volumes to Venice, where many of them are still preserved in the Marciana Library.

With Greek texts available practically all over Italy, the teaching of Greek ceased to be limited to Florence, while a large number of Greek authors was soon made available in Latin. In Florence, after Chrysoloras's departure, Greek continued to be taught with very few breaks; and already during the first half of the fifteenth century there were courses at Venice, Padua, Ferrara, Bologna, and Rome, as well as in other towns. It would, however, be incorrect to assume that Greek was being taught continuously in these cities during the fifteenth century, for this was certainly not so. A teacher might work for some years in one place and then move to another, and several years might elapse before a successor was found. Moreover, because of the reputation of a particular teacher, some students chose to learn their Greek away from home, even though facilities were available in their own town. Students from all parts of Italy flocked to Ferrara when Guarino was teaching there (1429–60), and the same happened at the school of Vittorino da Feltre (1373–1446) at Mantua. Alessandro Farnese, the future Pope Paul III, left Rome in 1487 in order to learn Greek in Florence, while in 1492 Pietro Bembo (1470–1547) went from his native Venice to far-away Messina to receive tuition in Greek from the celebrated Constantine Lascaris. It must be emphasized, however, that in spite of all this activity it was still exceptional in fifteenth-century Italy for a man to know Greek. It was only during the sixteenth century that Greek became a more usual feature of humanist education.

The main activity of Greek scholars in fifteenth-century Italy was the turning of texts into Latin. Medieval translations from the Greek had been strictly utilitarian and made with a view to the advancement of theology, philosophy, and science. History and literature in general were passed by. A utilitarian trend is still noticeable, it is true, in the choices of fifteenth-century translators. But their horizons were broad enough to include the works of historians and, in exceptional cases, even some poets other than Homer, such as Hesiod and Theocritus. On the other hand, the Greek tragic poets—after Pilatus's Latin rendering of a play by Euripides, which incidentally never circulated—remained untranslated until the early sixteenth century when Erasmus made a version of two more of the plays of Euripides.

Even the greatest fifteenth-century humanists did not

disdain the labour of translation. Bruni translated extensively from Plato, Aristotle, and Plutarch; Poggio turned to Diodorus and Xenophon, Decembrio to Plato and Appian; Valla chose Herodotus and Thucydides; Ermolao Barbaro the Younger, Themistius; Politian, Herodian and Epictetus. Among the Greek refugees, Theodor Gaza prepared Latin texts of Aristotle, while George of Trebizond produced versions of Plato, Aristotle, and some of the Greek fathers. But the greatest translator of the century was Marsilio Ficino (1433–1498) who turned the whole of Plato into Latin. Several of these humanist versions were of texts which had already been translated during the Middle Ages; and as a comparison with Bruni's Latin rendering of the *Ethics* and *Politics* shows, the new Aristotle proved to be little more than a revision of earlier versions in a style more consonant with humanist rhetoric. Unlike the medieval translators, with their painfully close following of the letter of the text, the humanists often incorporated their flamboyant rhetoric into the texts under the delusion that they were thus conveying more faithfully the spirit of the original.

The rediscovery of the ancient world, the new view of classical studies, as well as the methods of scholastic philosophy, were all instrumental in stimulating and developing a new critical approach. The Middle Ages had lacked historical sense and seemed unable to detect even the grossest anachronisms. A typical example is furnished by the thirteenth-century Florentine chronicle by Malespini, in which Catiline's wife is depicted hearing mass in the Fiesole parish church, more than fifty years before the birth of Christ. With humanism this was no longer possible, except in art and in popular literature. Fifteenth-century pictures representing scenes from classical mythology or ancient history, or even from the Bible, are commonly peopled with characters in Quattrocento attire, and even Dürer did not hesitate to paint Christ going to Calvary surrounded by the lansquenets of the Emperor Charles V.

Petrarch, on the other hand, had shown remarkable historical sense and critical insight in his textual and historical work. It was left to Lorenzo Valla (1407–1457) to show what humanist criticism could achieve, about seventy years after Petrarch's death.

A legend which circulated during the Middle Ages related how the Emperor Constantine had been struck with leprosy and healed by Pope St. Sylvester, whereupon the grateful emperor presented Rome and its surrounding territory to the Pope and transferred the capital of the Empire to Byzantium, which was henceforth called Constantinople. This legend originated from a document, purporting to record this gift, but almost certainly fabricated in the Papal Chancery in the ninth century to provide a legal backing for the temporal power of the Roman Pontiffs. This document, known as the Donation of Constantine, was violently denounced during the later Middle Ages. Dante and Walther von der Vogelweide thundered against it in verse. It was even claimed that at the very moment of the donation a voice was heard from heaven saying that poison had entered the Church of God. Yet no one had seriously challenged its authenticity before Lorenzo Valla. He scrutinized the text of the Donation and found, among other anachronisms, that its Latin did not conform with the usage of Constantine's time and that some towns mentioned in it had not yet been founded in the fourth century A.D. Thus he was able to prove beyond reasonable doubt that the Donation was spurious.

Valla's critical powers were also focussed upon other texts which had not fallen under suspicion before. He exposed as fictitious the correspondence between the philosopher Seneca and St. Paul, which had been in circulation at least since the time of St. Jerome, and dealt a similar blow to the Greek theological treatises, believed to have been written by Denys the Areopagite, which he showed could not possibly have been the work of a contemporary of St. Paul's. His critical daring reached its peak in his annotations on the New

Testament, where he subjected the Vulgate text to a searching criticism, furnishing by reference to the Greek original and to the writings of the early Fathers a series of corrections to the Holy Writ itself.

Critical methods no less striking were introduced into archaeological and historical studies by Flavio Biondo (1392–1463). In a sense one can say that Biondo 'invented' the Middle Ages, for he was the first to speak of a 'media antiquitas' starting in the year A.D. 412, when the Roman Empire was divided into eastern and western halves. As a historian he showed how sources could be used critically, while with his *Italia Illustrata* he gave the earliest example of historical geography. His greatest achievement, however, was his *Roma Instaurata*, in which he presented a reconstruction of Ancient Rome based on literary sources, on what he had discovered from personal study of the archeological remains, and on evidence from inscriptions, coins, and even medieval documents. He also inaugurated the study of Roman institutions in his *De Roma triumphante*.

Valla and Biondo succeeded in establishing a new and fruitful tradition. Valla's *Elegantiae* dominated grammatical and rhetorical studies in fifteenth-century Italy and sixteenth-century Western Europe, while Biondo set the style of antiquarian studies for a century. As a textual critic, Valla had two equals: Angelo Poliziano, or Politian as we call him, and Ermolao Barbaro the Younger. But they flourished two generations after him and brought their powers to bear on fields more restricted and certainly less controversial.

Politian (1454-1494), whose achievement as the greatest fifteenth-century Italian poet belongs to another chapter, devoted his exceptional critical insight to the interpretation and elucidation of classical texts ranging from Aristotle to Justinian's *Digest*. The *Sylvae* of Politian, which were inaugural lectures in Latin verse to his yearly course on classical authors in the University of Florence, combine the acumen of the critic with the imagination of the poet. As a scholar his masterpiece was, however, his *Miscellanea*, a collection of short dissertations on controversial or obscure points of classical scholarship. The first instalment of the *Miscellanea* (*Centuria Prima*) was published in Florence in 1489 and proved immediately successful. So much so that the secretary of the Duke of Milan, who happened to be in Florence at the time, found it impossible to get served in a shop because the assistants were so absorbed in reading Politian's work. A second instalment of the *Miscellanea* (*Centuria Secunda*) was left incomplete at Politian's death and only rediscovered a few years ago.

The dissertations in the *Miscellanea* dealt with points of scholarship such as the correct spelling of a Latin name, e.g. Vergilius or Virgilius, the meaning of a word, e.g. 'Entelecheia', or the elucidation of a particularly difficult passage in an ancient author. In reaching his solutions, Politian ransacked the Greek and Latin classics, considered and weighed the various manuscript readings, perused early textual commentaries, and queried the evidence of ancient inscriptions and coins. In all this he revealed himself as the greatest classical scholar of his time.

Among his contemporaries, the only one who came near him in learning and critical insight was the Venetian patrician, Ermolao Barbaro the Younger (1453–1493). Barbaro had, in addition, a strong interest in philosophy. His two main subjects of study were Aristotle's philosophy and the text of Pliny's *Natural History*. We shall see in a later chapter how Barbaro was convinced that the study of the philosopher needed radical rethinking. As a textual critic, he achieved fame with his *Castigationes Plinianae*, which appeared in Rome in 1492–3, and consisted of a series of emendations and explanations of some five thousand obscure or corrupt passages in Pliny's *Natural History*. The *Castigationes* is one of the great masterpieces in the history of classical scholarship, and its quality was perceived at once by his contemporaries. His early death in 1493 was rightly regarded as a calamity.

Barbaro and Politian were the heralds of a new scholarship, which made the efforts of Valla and his followers appear old-fashioned and superficial. But the new values fostered by humanism would have been restricted to only a very limited circle had it not been for the timely invention of printing, just when the Renaissance was beginning to reveal itself in all its glory. Between 1465 and 1473 all the major Latin classics were made available in print and in most cases in texts edited by the best humanistic talent available. Humanists also began to recast their lectures on ancient authors and publish them as commentaries, while their own poems, treatises, etc., enjoyed a circulation unheard of before.

Humanism conditioned every aspect of what we now call the Renaissance. Besides developing a new type of criticism and new standards of taste and aesthetic appreciation, it led to a new conception of the world. Close study of the ancient geographers led to new discoveries. To the geographies of Ptolemy and Strabo, as well as to the studies of cosmographers like Pierre d'Ailly and Paolo dal Pozzo Toscanelli, can be traced the discovery of America. The yearning of the humanists after classical antiquity found its counterpart in a longing for a return to the ideals of the early Church. Hebrew for the early reformers became what Greek had been for the humanists. The revival of classical learning was thus followed by a revival of Christian learning. One did not, however, exclude the other. Valla was interested in sacred as well as secular texts, just as a century before him Petrarch had studied the works of St. Augustine as sedulously as those of Cicero. It was, however, only in Erasmus that we find the first Christian humanist who was also an outstanding classical scholar.

Finally, humanism led to the creation of new literary forms. The resurrection of ancient types of poetry and prose stimulated the creation of new ones in the spoken tongues. In fact, in less than a century humanism changed the whole literary complexion of Italy, and in less than two centuries, that of Western Europe. It was really a switching from authority to freedom, so that henceforth nothing was to be accepted without being subject to scrutiny. Yet authority did not vanish altogether from literature. Imitation in the shape of Ciceronianism in Latin prose and Petrarchism in vernacular poetry remained virtually unchallenged until the second quarter of the sixteenth century. Then the first was laughed away by Erasmus, and the second was mercilessly parodied by Berni and his friends. In much the same way Rabelais had made such outrageous fun of scholasticism that it was no longer possible to find room for it in the universities.

# 4

# Platonism and Aristotelianism

BROADLY speaking, medieval thought means Aristotle and
Renaissance thought means Plato. It is true that Platonism
exerted some influence during the medieval period, while
the study and interpretation of Aristotle were by no means
extinct during the Renaissance. Yet it is equally true that
Plato reached the height of his popularity in fifteenth-
century Florence, whereas Aristotle had done so in
thirteenth-century Paris.

Although few of Plato's actual writings were known to
medieval Western Europe, some of his thought had been
transmitted through other writers and thus made available
to Western thinkers. St. Augustine's claim that Plato's
theory of a universe formed by a God was not against
Christian dogma had not been forgotten, while the writings
of late Roman classical writers such as Apuleius and
Macrobius, which were permeated with Platonism, had also
contributed to the transmission of Platonic thought. Here a
special role was played by Apuleius, whose *De Platone et
eius dogmate* and *De Deo Socratis* provided invaluable
summaries of what Plato had stood for.

To late antiquity belonged also the Latin translation of
the *Timaeus* by Chalcidius, and this was for many centuries
the only Platonic dialogue available to a West which had
forgotten Greek. Even later, when the Roman Empire in
the West had been replaced by the Gothic monarchy of
Theodoric (whom the Italians consigned to the darkest hell
and the Germans turned into a national hero), Boethius

(480?–524 or 525) sought refuge in Platonism, and wrote under its inspiration his *De consolatione philosophiae*, while waiting for the executioner in a dungeon at Pavia. In the same period a platonizing divine wrote a series of treatises in Greek, the most famous of which dealt with the nature and orders of angels. The name of this theologian has not survived, but his writings were believed for many centuries to be the work of Denys the Areopagite, and as documents of the apostolic age they enjoyed great popularity and authority. Finally, as early as the ninth century, the Dionysian texts were turned into Latin by Hilduin, Abbot of Saint-Denis, and their strong Platonizing element proved most influential. Thus the Platonism of John Scotus Eriugena, the great ninth-century philosopher, derived in part from the pseudo-Dionysus, of whose writings he also prepared a new translation.

The vitality of medieval Platonism is seen most clearly in the school of Chartres during the twelfth century. At Chartres the *Timaeus*, naturally in Chalcidius's Latin text, was sedulously studied. Moreover, one of the Chartres masters, William of Conches, wrote a commentary on it which became at once a set book in the teaching of natural philosophy. Thierry of Chartres also devoted himself to the study of Plato. And just when the school of Chartres had reached its zenith two dialogues of Plato, the *Phaedo* and the *Menon*, were turned into Latin in Norman Sicily by Henry Aristippus, Archdeacon of Catania.

An even more powerful Platonic influence was exerted during the thirteenth century by the *Liber de Pomo*, an Arabic imitation of the *Phaedo* which had been turned into Latin for Manfredi, King of Sicily (d. 1266) and was already a prescribed book in the University of Paris as early as 1255. Again in the thirteenth century the Flemish Dominican William of Moerbeke (1215?–1286), St. Thomas Aquinas's friend and companion, contributed versions of writings by Proclus, one of the most important interpreters of Plato.

49

Under these and similar influences Plato began to be openly preferred to Aristotle. Already Petrarch had placed Plato at the head of philosophers and owned Latin texts of the *Phaedo* and the *Timaeus*. Moreover, he possessed a bulky manuscript containing eighteen of Plato's dialogues in the original Greek text, the extent of his pride in this volume being matched only by his inability to read it. None the less, he fancied himself as a philosopher. So also did his spiritual heir, Coluccio Salutati, whose moral treatises, none the less, are quite valueless. But Salutati was at least responsible for having induced Emanuel Chrysoloras to come over to Florence in 1397. As we have seen, Chrysoloras really initiated the study of Greek in Florence. With the assistance of Uberto Decembrio, he also translated Plato's *Republic* into Latin, thus making this most important dialogue available to those who had no Greek.

Several of Chrysoloras's pupils took to translating Greek classical writings, chiefly Lucian and Plutarch. But a translation of the *Phaedo* also was made in 1404–5 by Leonardo Bruni, and this was soon followed by versions of other dialogues. What particularly attracted Bruni to Plato was the fact that his doctrines bore some resemblance to those of Christianity. For a time he considered Plato superior to Aristotle as a philosopher, though this was an opinion he did not hold for long.

Thanks mainly to Chrysoloras and Bruni, early-fifteenth-century Florence became fully aware of Plato. What did most, however, to turn it into the main centre of Platonism in Western Europe was the Council of Florence, which led to the short-lived Act of Union between the Greek and Latin Churches in 1439. Among the members of the Byzantine delegation at the Council was Gemistos Pletho, the greatest living exponent of the Byzantine Platonist tradition. Pletho, whose eloquence and powers of persuasion seem to have been of a very high order, deeply impressed the Florentine humanists. Here was a man to whom Platonism was a living reality: a way of life, and not merely a doctrine.

And, indeed, Pletho aimed at setting up Platonism as a universal system. On the basis of Proclus's writings, he even went so far as to make an allegorical interpretation of the ancient gods. That this led eventually to charges of paganism being levelled against him is perhaps scarcely surprising, but whether there was really anything in the charges we cannot now judge.

Pletho's Platonism, at least, found fertile ground in Florence. Cosimo de Medici the Elder (1389–1464), the wealthy banker who really ruled the city, himself felt the fascination of Plato. In the University, John Argyropoulos, one of the many Byzantines who had found a new home in the West, introduced the study of Plato at the academic level. In fact, his lectures, though nominally on Aristotle's *Nicomachean Ethics*, really dealt as much with Plato as they did with Aristotle. His aim was to show that the doctrines of the two philosophers were in harmony and complementary to each other. Another Byzantine exile, George of Trebizond, reacted by violently attacking Plato in his *Comparationes philosophorum Aristotelis et Platonis*. The defence was taken up by the Greek-born Cardinal Bessarion with his *In calumniatorem Platonis*. In this treatise every point put forward by George against Plato was refuted, though without any attempt to diminish Aristotle's stature. What Bessarion set out to prove was not only that Plato was a greater philosopher than Aristotle but how close he had been to Christianity, a view supported by the ample use of Plato's writings made by the Church Fathers.

The Platonism of Bessarion was shared by his friend Cardinal Nicholas of Cusa, the greatest speculative mind of the fifteenth century, whose philosophical thought was permeated by a Platonism tempered by Proclus, the pseudo-Dionysius, and Thierry of Chartres. It was, however, left to a less profound thinker, Marsilio Ficino (1433–1499), to become the main interpreter and inspiration of Renaissance Platonism. Although he had been the pupil of an Aristotelian, Niccolò Tignosi of Foligno, it was not long before he turned to Plato. An early work, his *Institutiones ad Platonicam disciplinam*, written in 1456, is now lost. Intensive reading of neoplatonist writers led him to prepare a Latin version of the *Pimander* (ascribed to Hermes Trismegistos) in 1463. In the same year he embarked upon a Latin translation of the whole *Corpus Platonicum*. This tremendous task was finally accomplished in 1477, and was accompanied by a life of Plato, also in Latin. Ficino was not, however, simply a translator and expositor. In a succession of treatises he endeavoured to do for Plato what St. Thomas Aquinas had done for Aristotle. In his *Theologia Platonica seu de immortalitate animarum* he went beyond mere exposition of Plato's philosophy; he expounded a neoplatonism of his own and sought to prove the existence of a hierarchy with God as the supreme being. Platonism also played a preponderant role in his *De Christiana Religione*, in which he set out to defend Christianity against Moslems and Jews. According to his presentation of the Platonic doctrine (in a commentary on the *Symposion*), love became a craving for beauty, which in turn led to a desire for God, conceived as infinite love of infinite beauty. Like Bessarion, Ficino regarded Plato as a forerunner of Christianity. And Plato remained to the end his ruling passion, a passion which found concrete expression in his Platonic Academy, where he gathered all the best elements in the intellectual life of Florence.

The impact of Ficino was particularly powerful upon Giovanni Pico della Mirandola (1463–1494) who was in Florence from 1488 until his death. Pico, celebrated as the author of nine hundred theses embracing the whole of knowledge, had started upon his philosophic career as a student of scholastic philosophy and a devotee of Averrois, but under the influence of Ficino he turned aside from Aristotle to Plato. In his *De ente et uno*, like others before him, he sought to reconcile the philosophy of Plato with that of Aristotle, while his study of the Jewish *Kabbalah* moved him to harmonize it with Christian theology and associate it with Christian tradition. The doctrines of Plato and Aristotle figure prominently in his *Heptaplus*, a seven-fold interpretation of the Mosaic cosmogony; and Platonism was the chief inspiration of his *De hominis dignitate* in which he vigorously asserted the inherent dignity of man in the universe. As time went on, however, Pico's Platonism inclined more and more towards mysticism.

After his death Renaissance Italian Platonism followed two different paths, the philosophical and the literary. During the sixteenth century Plato's dialogues became university set books in the study of philosophy, and the mantle of Ficino and Pico fell upon the Augustinian friar, later Cardinal, Egidio of Viterbo (1469–1532), who incidentally shared Pico's taste for the *Kabbalah*. Egidio's commentary on the *Sentences* of Peter the Lombard 'ad mentem Platonis' illustrated his introduction of Platonism into theology. It was left, however, to Francesco Patrizi (1529–1597) to speak the last words of Renaissance Platonism in his *Nuova filosofia*. Whereas philosophical Platonism was almost entirely expressed in Latin, literary Platonism showed itself particularly strong in vernacular writings. Already Lorenzo de Medici the Magnificent (1449–1492) had coloured his *Selve* and his love lyrics with Platonic doctrines, while his *Altercazione* was a versified exposition of the Platonist doctrine of happiness. Platonism as understood by Ficino and Pico proved even stronger in writers such as Nesi and Verino. Nesi's *Oraculum de novo saeculo*, a poem inspired by the ideas of Savonarola, is also much influenced by Pico. The mysticism of Pico, however, found its highest poetic expression in the *Canzone d'Amore* of Girolamo Benivieni.

The death of Ficino in 1499 also marks the end of the academy of which he had been the life and soul. Its successor in Florence was the group of scholars, men of letters, and philosophers who met in the Rucellai Gardens, the so-called Orti Oricellari, among whom Francesco Cattani da Diacceto particularly distinguished himself. Strangely enough, his *Tre libri d'Amore*, though written within the tradition established by Ficino, is in many ways closer to Pico's thought. On the other hand, Ficino's theory of love is to be felt strongly in the *Asolani* of Pietro Bembo, first published in 1505, and is also present in the *Dialoghi d'Amore* of Leone Ebreo, the work which became the love code of the high Renaissance. Renaissance Platonism eventually became an important element in vernacular literature. Aristotelianism, on the other hand, affected literature only when Aristotle's *Poetics* began to be appreciated; and this, despite the long tradition of Aristotelian studies in the West, was not before the sixteenth century.

Medieval Aristotelianism can be traced back to Boethius, whom we know to have turned at least two of Aristotle's works into Latin. In contrast, St. Augustine, who contributed so much to the transmission of Platonic thought, seems hardly to have been affected by Aristotle. Those who really spread the knowledge of Aristotle's thought were, however, the Arabs. Their scholars, working in the Middle East and in Spain, translated most of his works into their own language and produced commentaries and paraphrases, as well as treatises dominated by his philosophy. The results of their activities reached the West after being translated into Latin in Spain during the twelfth and thirteenth centuries. Among these Arabic interpreters of Aristotle, Avicenna (980–1037) and Averrois (1126–1198) proved especially popular among Western thinkers. Indeed, Averrois acquired such prestige that he became known as 'Magnus Commentator', while Dante placed him in his 'nobile castello' together with the greatest sages and heroes of antiquity.

Just when these Latin texts were finding their way across the Pyrenees the original Greek text of Aristotle began to receive attention from Western translators. Already during the twelfth century a scholar like James of Venice had picked up enough Greek in Constantinople to undertake a translation of some of Aristotle's treatises on logic. And it was not long before the ecclesiastical authorities became preoccupied by the growing popularity of the Aristotelian writings and what they stood for. The so-called *Libri Naturales* aroused particular suspicion, so much so that in 1210 their use was forbidden in Paris by the Papal Legate, and again in 1231 by Pope Gregory IX. Such bans did not, however, stop the teachers or translators. During the first half of the thirteenth century Robert Grosseteste (d. 1253), the great Bishop of Lincoln, who had learnt Aristotle's language from Greek scholars in his household, was one of the several people who latinized Aristotelian treatises. But the most prolific translator of the century proved to be the Flemish Dominican, William of Moerbeke, who was encouraged by St. Thomas Aquinas to translate practically the whole of Aristotle's works. Even by the middle of the thirteenth century Aristotle had become the main basis of philosophical instruction in Paris, where his doctrines proved particularly influential in the faculty of medicine. It was St. Thomas Aquinas, himself a Paris master, who set out to reconcile Aristotle with Christian theology, giving the Greek philosopher a prestige scarcely inferior to that of a Church Father. Nor was the interpretation of Aristotle by Averrois overlooked. Some Paris masters, like Siger of Brabant and Boethius of Dacia, took over Averrois' approach and launched what became known as Latin Averroism—that is, a materialist interpretation of Aristotle which included a belief in the eternity of the world and in the unity of intellect in all men, but left no room for individual immortality.

By the end of the thirteenth century both Paris and Oxford were dominated by Aristotle. At Italian universities, on the other hand, the teaching still included only rhetoric, law, and medicine. Theology and philosophy were taught elsewhere, in the houses of the mendicant orders (the Dominicans and Franciscans), and it was to them that Dante resorted for theological and philosophical instruction. For Dante himself Aristotle was 'Il maestro di color che sanno', 'the teacher of those who know', and Aristotelianism permeated his main works.

It was not until the fourteenth century that Aristotle dominated philosophical teaching in Italy also. In the absence of theological faculties (at any rate, before the late fourteenth century) those of medicine became the centres of Italian Aristotelianism. This Aristotelianism was often tinged with either Averroism or with Occamism, a revived form of Nominalism which holds that nothing general exists except 'names'. The theological schools of the religious orders, on the other hand, followed the line of St. Thomas Aquinas or Duns Scotus.

From the outset, humanists had shown hostility to scholastic learning and all it stood for. Yet even Petrarch was always ready to concede that Aristotle was far better than his translators or commentators. Humanist opposition to Aristotle was really inspired by considerations of rhetoric and by objections to the indifferent style of the schoolmen's Latin. The schoolmen in their turn often looked with suspicion at humanist activities. It is not surprising therefore that when the humanists took over Aristotle they took over the Aristotle of Byzantine tradition, not of the schoolmen.

With the rise of humanist Greek studies in the early fifteenth century, the Greek text of Aristotle soon commanded the attention of Leonardo Bruni himself. When he forsook Plato for Aristotle he made Latin translations of the *Nicomachean Ethics* and the *Politics*. These became accepted as the standard texts, even though they were (as has been said earlier) little more than rhetorical revisions of the older translations.

Thus, even during the decades when Platonism was the leading intellectual influence in Florence, Aristotelianism still flourished there. But among the humanists Aristotle was approached more as a literary than a philosophical writer, as we may judge from the lectures by John Argyropoulos on the *Nicomachean Ethics* in which he attempted to reconcile Aristotle with Plato, or from Politian's course on the *Analytica Priora*. Perhaps the man who strove hardest of all to reconcile Platonism and Aristotelianism was Pico della Mirandola, though his efforts proved in the end no more successful than his other more ambitious schemes.

The strongholds of Aristotelianism in Italy were Padua and to a lesser extent Bologna. It was, for instance, in Padua that an interest in Aristotle's Greek commentators was first aroused; a pioneer in this direction was the Venetian patrician, Ermolao Barbaro the Younger, whose Latin version of Themistius gave a fresh impetus to Aristotelian studies. Barbaro was followed by his friend Girolamo Donato (1457–1511), who translated the *De Anima* of Alexander of Aphrodisia. Previously, Nicoletto Vernia (*c.* 1420–1499) had been the greatest exponent in Padua of what might be termed the Averroist approach. Until the intervention of Pietro Barozzi, Bishop of Padua, Vernia had taught among other things the doctrine of the unity of intellect, which was tantamount to a denial of the survival of the individual soul (though Aristotle is, in fact, ambiguous on the subject). It remained for Pietro Pomponazzi (1462–1525), who knew no Greek, to prove himself the greatest Renaissance exponent of Aristotle. His was an Aristotelianism which emphasized the paramount position of man and claimed that the practical intellect was much more important than the speculative one, so far as happiness was concerned. The Stoic doctrine of fate also held strong attractions for Pomponazzi, and in his lectures he defended it strenuously against Alexander of Aphrodisia.

It was unfortunate that even professional philosophers like Vernia and Pomponazzi had to rely entirely upon Latin translations, many of them inaccurate medieval ones. Even the few humanist versions that existed did not invariably render the thought of the great philosopher with accuracy. This was a matter which particularly concerned Ermolao Barbaro the Younger and led him to advocate a twofold solution of the problem: on the one hand, to publish as widely as possible the Greek text, so that it could be obtained without difficulty; on the other, to re-translate the whole of Aristotle with the utmost accuracy, so as to remove the possibility of misinterpretation.

Ermolao Barbaro the Younger did all he could to further his vision of a new Aristotelianism, but he was deeply involved in diplomatic activities on behalf of the Venetian Republic; and his subsequent break with Venice through his acceptance of the patriarchate of Aquileia (bestowed on him by Pope Innocent VIII), and his untimely death in 1493, seemed to have brought his schemes to nothing. But not completely, for we can trace to them the origins of the Aldine edition of the Greek text of Aristotle, which appeared in five volumes between 1495 and 1498. Again, it was Ermolao's activity which eventually in 1497 made possible the appointment of Leonico Tomeo to lecture in Padua on the Greek text. As for the prospect of a new translation, although this was taken up again at Alcalá by the Spanish Cardinal Ximenes during the second decade of the sixteenth century, once more nothing came of it owing to the Cardinal's death.

During the sixteenth century Aristotelianism continued to dominate the universities of Italy, indeed of Europe, and even in the days of Galileo it was far from having been eliminated from their 'curricula'. It was also during the sixteenth century that Aristotle came to exert a powerful influence on literature. The Latin translation of his *Poetics*, made during the thirteenth century, was known to several humanists. As for the original Greek text, it is known that Politian possessed a copy, but he does not appear to have taken much notice of its doctrines. Yet it was not until the middle of the sixteenth century that the real discovery of the *Poetics* took place. The first commentary on it, by Robertelli, appeared as late as 1548, so that it is only in the second half of the Cinquecento that we find the full impact of Aristotelian doctrine on literary criticism and on the controversies raging over the dead Ariosto and the still-living Tasso.

Platonism and Aristotelianism both belonged as much to the Middle Ages as they did to the Renaissance. Until the sixteenth century what really distinguished humanist Aristotelianism from medieval was merely that the humanists had a better knowledge of Greek. In Platonism the situation was different. Here the Renaissance provided direct knowledge and interpretation from what had hitherto been indirect knowledge. As far as their thought was concerned, Plato and Aristotle held a position like that of Cicero in rhetoric and Virgil in poetry. They, and they alone, supplied the supreme examples. There was this difference, though, that after the debates between Bessarion and George of Trebizond there was scarcely any outstanding conflict between the devotees of the two philosophers. The Aristotelians were also Platonists and the Platonists were also Aristotelians. The dream of Pico della Mirandola about the reconciliation of the two systems was effected in practice, if not quite in theory, during the Renaissance.

# 5

# The new literary forms

THE Renaissance witnessed the rise of new literary forms in vernacular literature. Some of these were the direct result of humanism; others, though not directly indebted to it, were none the less the outcome of the new literary climate which humanism more than anything else had brought about.

Prejudice against the use of the vernacular in literary works took some time to die out in Italy. During the first two decades of the fourteenth century, when Dante was writing his supreme masterpiece, humanists and grammarians were convinced that the powers of expression of the spoken tongue were limited. It was, therefore, scarcely surprising that Giovanni del Virgilio, a teacher of grammar at Bologna, should reproach Dante for not having written the *Divine Comedy* in Latin. To be without Latin was equivalent to being illiterate. In fact, until Dante proved otherwise, it was believed that the vernacular could not express the finer shades of philosophical speculation, simply because of its limited vocabulary and lack of cultural background.

Dante's confidence in the excellence of his native language is already evident in the youthful *Vita Nuova*, which was completed in all probability about 1293. It was, however, in the *De Vulgari Eloquentia* and the *Convivio*, both belonging to the period 1304–7, that he first set out his views plainly. Finally, in the *Divine Comedy* he demonstrated what the despised spoken tongue could achieve in the hands of a writer of genius. None the less, he never ceased to believe in the superiority of Latin. More than a generation after Dante, Petrarch still entertained no doubts in the matter. Although he spent much of life in the composition of those Italian poems of his which are, ironically enough, the only part of his literary production read nowadays, his greatest efforts went into the writing of his Latin works. It was with them that he expected to achieve immortality, and he dismissed his Italian lyrics as *nugellae*—that is, 'trifles'. On the other hand, when he died he was still busy revising Italian poems written several decades before, so that his declared contempt for this side of his work may not have been entirely sincere.

Boccaccio, too, left writings both in Latin and in Italian, and again it is only one of his Italian works, the *Decameron*, that is read nowadays. Though a humanist, Boccaccio wrote extensively in Italian prose as well as verse, whereas the only piece of Italian prose by Petrarch which we know is a letter, and a very short one at that. But, then, Petrarch's prejudices against the vernacular were not shared by Boccaccio, who, unlike Petrarch, had a boundless admiration for Dante. Humanism, on the whole, sided with Petrarch rather than with Boccaccio. In the early fifteenth century there were scholars, in Florence of all places, who declared that Dante was fit to be read only by cobblers and bakers, and that Boccaccio was ignorant of 'grammar'—that is, of Latin. Fortunately, such views were not universal. Dante did not lack admirers, biographers, and commentators among the humanists, Bruni and Landino among them. Nor were the Italian poems of Petrarch or the stories of the *Decameron* neglected. Several humanists chose to write both in Latin and in Italian; Leon Battista Alberti, Filelfo, Politian, Bembo, and others achieved literary distinction in both languages. Yet even during the sixteenth century the old prejudice against the literary use of the vernacular had not altogether died out. When the Emperor Charles V and Pope Clement VII were in Bologna in 1529 they were treated to an oration by the humanist Romolo Amaseo, which was a long-drawn-out tirade against the vernacular tongue.

Again, Benedetto Varchi (1503–1565) recalled in his *Ercolano* how, in his youth, parents and teachers forbade children to read anything in the vernacular, and how he himself was nearly expelled from school for having been caught reading the Italian poems of Petrarch.

The gradual acceptance of the Italian vernacular as a literary language led to the development of new literary forms. Some of them were merely adaptations of genres already used in Latin; some had their roots, at least, in Latin forms; others were modifications of literary genres with an already long vernacular tradition behind them. In the writing of history the medieval chronicle in Italy had found vernacular writers since the late thirteenth century. The same change from Latin to Italian came later in humanist historiography, inaugurated during the first half of the fifteenth century by Leonardo Bruni with his Latin history of Florence. Finally, in the sixteenth century, we find the two greatest achievements of the new historiography, Machiavelli's *Storie Fiorentine* and Guicciardini's *Storia d'Italia*, both in Italian.

Biography also acquired a new shape during the Renaissance. During the Middle Ages it had very seldom strayed beyond a strict recital of the lives of saints, popes, bishops, or great secular rulers. These consisted of a string of facts, enlivened with anecdotes and accounts of miracles. Even Petrarch's biographical works still conformed to medieval tradition; the same is true of Boccaccio's *De claris Mulieribus* and *De casibus virorum illustrium*, and of the lives of illustrious Florentines by Filippo Villani. Boccaccio, however, also gave us in his life of Dante the first modern biography.

This life, which Boccaccio chose to write in Italian, is encumbered with anecdotes, some as ancient as Herodotus and simply adapted to his hero. Yet Dante emerges as a living figure even though he is presented as the very personification of poetry. The biography of Dante by Leonardo Bruni, on the other hand, not only results from genuine research but also shows discernment in its use of sources.

Personal experiences and recollections dominate the biographies by Vespasiano da Bisticci, the Florentine bookseller who mostly wrote of distinguished persons met during his long career as a purveyor of manuscripts. What Vespasiano produced might be called popular biography. In more serious vein, Machiavelli created in his *Vita di Castruccio Castracani* a striking portrait of an early fourteenth-century despot.

Humanist biography had its ultimate roots in the *Lives* of Plutarch and Suetonius. Similarly, the humanist dialogue, both in Latin and in Italian, had direct classical origins. The Platonic dialogues had had many imitators, first in Greece, where Aristotle's lost dialogues were the most outstanding, and then in Rome, where Cicero and Seneca furnished the leading examples. Latin dialogues were also written during the Middle Ages, and humanists inevitably adopted this literary form as a means of expounding their opinions. Albertino Mussato's Latin dialogues are the earliest humanist specimens we have, but Petrarch's *Secretum*, in which he discusses his spiritual problems with St. Augustine, is perhaps the best known. As the Renaissance went on, dialogues began to appear in the vernacular also. The *Libri della Famiglia* by Leon Battista Alberti (1404–1472), written in an Italian strongly permeated with Latin, were set against a Florentine background and dealt with matters of immediate interest to Florentines. Bembo's *Asolani* dealt with Platonic love, while his *Prose della volgar lingua* debated the nature and usage of literary Italian and advocated an archaic language based on Petrarch for poetry and Boccaccio for prose. Among all these vernacular dialogues of the fifteenth and sixteenth centuries one became more famous than the rest: Castiglione's *Cortegiano*, a series of discussions which built up by stages the figure of the ideal Renaissance courtier.

All the literary forms so far examined were of learned origin. Less scholarly was the Italian 'novella' or short story, which made its first appearance during the second half of the thirteenth century. Behind the 'novella' stand the tale, the anecdote, and the 'fabliaux' or versified tales. As a genre, the 'fabliaux' found no direct followers in Italy. If we examine one of the earliest collections of short stories in Italian, the *Cento Novelle Antike*, commonly known as *Il Novellino*, we find that a substantial part consists of enlarged versions of anecdotes from classical antiquity, or of tales connected either with romantic legends or with recent personages. They are structurally reminiscent of the anecdotes in the Latin treatise of Valerius Maximus, whose immense popularity survived the Middle Ages, though not the Renaissance. But what in Valerius Maximus are purely anecdotes are now turned into recognizable short stories. The same is true of another Italian collection, the *Libro dei sette savi*, where (as in the *Decameron*, the *Canterbury Tales*, and the *Arabian Nights*) the stories are given the general setting of a particular occasion.

The short story in Italy had by no means fully developed by the end of the thirteenth century. It was Boccaccio who transformed the art of short-story writing beyond recognition. Under his hands the short story became both wider and deeper. It now became in some cases almost a short novel, and the unities of time and space which were commonly observed in the earlier collections were not necessarily obeyed.

The stories of the *Decameron*, like Chaucer's *Canterbury Tales*, point no moral. Boccaccio's Italian successor in the field of short-story writing, Franco Sacchetti, had not the wit and vitality of his predecessor, and felt it necessary to underline the message at the end of each of his 'novelle'. After the unexpected triumph of the *Decameron* it was inevitable that its imitations should seem pale reflections, even if they were not so far removed from their model as those wretched imitations of the *Divine Comedy* were from theirs. In fact, the major Quattrocento imitations of the *Decameron*, such as the *Novellino* of Masuccio Salernitano and the *Porrettane* of Sabadino degli Arienti, are not without merit, and at least succeed in giving an accurate picture of the contemporary scene. But we have to wait until Matteo Bandello (1485–1561) before we again find 'novelle' which are genuine works of art.

As we have noted, the distance between the 'novella' and the 'romance' occasionally narrowed. Some of Boccaccio's short stories are almost romances in miniature. Now romances, which Dante called 'prose di romanzi', were most popular during the later Middle Ages. They were essentially a French monopoly, and those written in German, Spanish, or Italian were so only in vocabulary and grammar. The majority draw their subject-matter from the Arthurian legend, the 'Arturi regis ambages pulcerrime' of Dante. There were also some which dealt with the matter of Troy or of Rome the Great, though their heroes or heroines did not differ much in outlook or behaviour from the Arthurian ones. A different kind of romance developed in late fifteenth-century Italy, when classical sources like the romance of Apuleius and the classical eclogue—still a living influence during the Middle Ages—were the starting-point for romances which created a make-believe world as an escape from the realities of an Italy on the verge of political catastrophe.

The *Arcadia* by Jacopo Sannazzaro (1455 or 1456–1530) inaugurated the pastoral romance and we shall return to this later. The fantastic novel began with the *Hypnerotomachia Poliphili* by the disreputable Dominican Francesco Colonna. First published in 1499, but very probably written some decades earlier, this work tells the amorous adventures of its hero and heroine, but it is burdened by the most suffocating erudition and probably the most cumbersome style and diction in the whole of Italian literature. Mercifully for Renaissance letters, Colonna's work found no imitators. The *Libro del Peregrino* by Jacopo Caviceo was a complicated love story, dedicated in 1508 to Lucretia Borgia, and intended to show under a veil of allegory the instability of fortune. In it, all the antiquarian flummery, which made the *Hypnerotomachia* so unwieldy and top heavy, has mercifully disappeared, yet without rendering the book any more palatable now. None the less, by the early sixteenth century the Italian Renaissance novel had reached its full development and was ready to cross the Alps.

Whereas the novel, or rather the romances which are its direct forerunners, had flourished during the later Middle Ages, one cannot say the same of secular dramatic literature. The Romans had taken over the drama of the Greeks without contributing anything of value on their own account. All that has survived is the tragedies of Seneca and the comedies of Plautus and Terence. Of these, only Seneca and Terence were known to the Middle Ages; Plautus had been neglected owing to the difficulty of his Latin. He was rediscovered only in the early fifteenth century.

Terence's comedies were a popular school text, even though he was believed to have written in prose, not verse. But they do not appear to have been imitated, apart from the Latin plays of a tenth-century Saxon nun named Hroswitha, or indeed performed before the Renaissance. They were merely read. Before the fourteenth century dramatic performances were restricted to mystery plays and farces. It was left to humanism to reveal new horizons.

Broadly speaking, medieval drama was religious; Renaissance drama was secular. There was renewed interest in Latin drama, and, thanks to Lovato Lovati, Seneca's tragedies became quite popular in Padua (it was here, incidentally, that their metres were first understood). As we have seen earlier, Mussato's *Ecerinis*, the first tragedy written since classical times, was based on Seneca. Its success was, however, literary and rhetorical rather than dramatic. It may have received one performance, but otherwise it was read as literature; so, too, were the late-fourteenth-century imitations of it, such as the *Achilles* or the tragedy on the fall of Antonio della Scala, Lord of Verona. This latter play was exceptional in dealing with a contemporary event, for throughout the fifteenth century the subject matter of tragedies was strictly classical on the Senecan pattern.

Gregorio Correr's *Progne* and Leonardo Dati's *Hiempsal*
are examples. But such plays aroused no particular enthusiasm, and it was not until the sixteenth century that tragedies
began to be written in Italian. These vernacular plays took
Sophocles as their model and Aristotle as their theorist.
Unity of time, place, and action became dramatic dogma and
dominated tragedies like Trissino's *Sofonisba*, Rucellai's
*Rosmunda*, and Alamanni's *Antigone*. A subsequent return
to Seneca produced a somewhat different style of tragedy,
which blended excessive sententiousness with an element of
horror. The *Orbecche* by Giraldi Cinthio and the *Canace* by
Sperone Speroni were typical of this new kind of drama,
which seems to have appealed to Italian audiences, just as it
would have done to the Elizabethan public.

For all this activity, the Italian Renaissance produced
not one tragedy worth reading today. With Machiavelli's
*Mandragola*, however, it gave us the greatest play in Italian
literature, indeed one of the greatest in European drama—
'the comedy of an age', as Villari said, 'of which Machiavelli's *Prince* is the tragedy'. Comedies in Latin verse had
been written in twelfth-century France, and Petrarch had
also written one, the *Philologia Philostrati*, now unfortunately
lost. These were mere versified tales, but were classed as
'comedies' because in medieval Latin 'comoedia' also meant
any literary narrative with a gloomy beginning and a happy
ending. For comedies in the more usual sense we have to
wait until the fifteenth century. Several humanists then
tried their hand at imitating Plautus and Terence, but the
efforts of Alberti, Vergerio, and Aeneas Sylvius Piccolomini
(later Pope Pius II, 1458–64) are significant only to the
literary historian.

Latin humanist comedies, in fact, show no development
from their Plautine and Terentian prototypes. It was only
when comedies began to be written in Italian that some
development took place. The already involved plots of
Plautus and Terence now became even more so with
Ariosto, and the treatment more obscene. The peak of

obscenity was reached by Cardinal Bernardo Dovizi da Bibbiena, the favourite of Pope Leo X, with *La Calandria*, a play which was first staged at the court of Urbino in 1513.

Even during the Renaissance there were signs of a reaction against the dominance of Plautus and Terence. The plays of Pietro Aretino, that most scurrilous of writers in an age not particularly noted for its moral standards, are not drawn from stereotyped models but attempt to portray everyday life. Perhaps this is because Aretino was without humanist culture. His plays certainly represent a move in the right direction in that they break away from tradition, but they were none the less failures. Despite the occasional brilliant scene and the striking characterization, they are now deservedly forgotten, along with the comparable plays of Giammaria Cecchi. It is only with the Paduan Ruzzante that we find a playwright who was able to contribute some real vitality. In fact, his plays already anticipate in several ways the 'Commedia dell 'Arte', and look ahead to a time when the Renaissance was a thing of the past, at any rate in Italy.

As a whole, Italian Renaissance drama would have been a pale shadow of the classical had it not been for the pastoral drama. The classical eclogues were versified dialogues between shepherds, who generally symbolized real people and whose conversations concealed hidden allusions. The genre, as we have seen, had never been forgotten, even during the Middle Ages, and Dante, Petrarch, and Boccaccio were among the authors of bucolic poems modelled upon those of Virgil. Again, mystery plays had also long been a tradition in Italy, and even sophisticated men of letters like Lorenzo de Medici the Magnificent (1449–1492), had not scorned to try their hand at them. In such plays and in the eclogues we may see the origin of the pastoral drama.

The earliest example is provided by Politian. He was pressed at short notice to write a play for performance at a princely feast in Mantua in 1480, and the result was his *Fabula di Orfeo*. He devised a dramatic structure with features from both the classical eclogue and the medieval mystery play, and introduced choruses which were closer to the 'canti carnascialeschi' (carnival songs) of Florence than to anything in Sophocles or Seneca. The *Fabula di Orfeo* led to the *Arcadia* of Sannazzaro, though this is a romance and not a play. And both of them were the direct ancestors of the *Sacrificio* by Agostino Beccari (1554), the first fully fledged pastoral drama. In Italy this dramatic form did not have a long life, but it included one major masterpiece, Tasso's *Aminta*, and a minor one, Guarini's *Pastor Fido*.

All in all, Italian Renaissance drama contributed strongly to the development of European drama, even if its lasting successes were few. Similarly, Italian poetic metres proved influential outside Italy. Though its name is derived from the Provençal 'sonet', meaning a short lyric, the sonnet was actually invented by the poets of the Sicilian court of the Emperor Frederick II (1194–1250). Two generations after the first sonnets had been written Dante showed in the *Vita Nuova* what lyric heights could be reached in the form. Two generations later again, Petrarch used the sonnet for most of his Italian lyrics and these had a great influence beyond the shores of Italy. By the sixteenth century, sonnets were being written almost everywhere in Western Europe. By then, too, the eight-line stanza, which had first appeared in Italy during the fourteenth century, and which Boiardo and Ariosto had used in their epics, had also become naturalized abroad, and was eventually adapted by Spenser to his own genius. Another typically Italian metre, the 'terza rima', which Dante had chosen for his masterpiece, did not prove so acceptable. Although it was used by Petrarch in his *Trionfi* and by Boccaccio in his *Amorosa Visione*, it then virtually fell into disuse. By the sixteenth century it was seldom employed except in satire.

Besides popularizing the sonnet outside Italy, Petrarch dominated the Western European love lyric. His introspective poetry, with its flamboyant imagery, subtle conceits, and highly polished diction, by which the most intimate moods were translated into lyric terms, proved irresistible; even as late as the nineteenth century a great poet like Leopardi revealed clear signs of Petrarch's influence.

The epic poetry of Renaissance Europe also found its models in Italy. The medieval epic was a French creation, and conditions in Italy at that time were not favourable to the composition of poems like the *Chanson de Roland*. When eventually the French epic crossed into north Italy the local dialects proved close enough to French for the recitations by itinerant minstrels to be intelligible to popular audiences. Similarly the French Arthurian romances proved very popular in Italy. But the blood and thunder of the 'Chansons de Geste' found appreciative audiences in the 'piazza' (Poggio relates how a Milanese listener was so moved by a recital of Roland's death heard in a square that when he got back home he was unable to touch his dinner): whereas the Arthurian romances appealed exclusively to the upper classes. Those who have read Dante's *Inferno* may recall how the fate of Paolo and Francesca was sealed in the pages of the romance of Lancelot.

Both epics and romances found translators and imitators in Italy. But during the fifteenth century epic poetry underwent a change in Italy. The subject-matter of the 'Chansons de Geste' may have appealed to French patriotism and Christian feeling, but Italian readers merely wished to be entertained. New episodes, digressions, and even new characters now appeared in epic poems, until they lost most of their original character. They became chivalric romances, 'romanzi di cavalleria', in which the old epic matter was fused with elements from the romances. The heroes, in particular, ceased to behave as medieval knights and became typically Renaissance characters. The high seriousness of true epic was now weakened by the introduction of comic episodes and accounts of the course of true or untrue love. The outlook of the Florentine middle class, whose wit and sense of fun is so strikingly caught by Boccaccio in the *Decameron*, colours the *Morgante Maggiore* of Luigi Pulci

(1432–1484). Here Charlemagne is already 'il re Carlone', the character who has given to the Italian language the expression 'alla Carlona', i.e. clumsily. Pulci was, after all, a Florentine bourgeois, whose life and ideals were those of the 'piazza' rather than of Ficino's Platonic Academy. Count Matteo Maria Boiardo (1441–1494), on the other hand, was a feudatory and courtier of the Duke of Ferrara. Hence his *Orlando Innamorato*, unfinished at his death, was peopled by late-fifteenth-century gentlemen, behaving more like Ferrarese courtiers than contemporaries of Charlemagne. The *Orlando Innamorato* represents the final surrender of the Arthurian romance to the 'Chanson de Geste', all in a typically Renaissance setting.

In general, Italian chivalric romance relegated the epic matter to the background. The wars of Charlemagne against the Moors no longer mattered; instead we have the amorous adventures of the knights and their encounters with monsters, sorcerers, damsels in distress, witches, and temptation. These Renaissance romances played a role similar to that of the modern novel or television: they were fiction, and their aim was to entertain. Though their final form was shaped by Boiardo, it was Ludovico Ariosto (1474–1533) whose work became known abroad. For although the *Orlando Innamorato* figured among Don Quixote's books which were burnt by the parish priest, it was the *Orlando Furioso* of Ariosto, with its boundless imagination and matchless poetry, that made the chivalric romance a European literary genre. After Ariosto, lack of imagination and slavish adherence to Aristotle delayed the appearance of another chivalric romance worth reading until the age of Tasso; no one today, for instance, would read for pleasure Trissino's *Italia liberata dai Goti* or Alamanni's *Avarchide*.

The new literary forms were among the most valuable contributions of Renaissance Italy to the literature of Europe. They had a lasting effect and but for them medieval literature would not have vanished altogether during the sixteenth century.

# 6

# Sannazzaro, Castiglione, Ariosto, Machiavelli

DURING the fifteenth century general taste turned from Petrarch's Latin writing to his Italian poems. Nothing reveals so clearly the switch from the classic to the spoken tongue which was steadily taking place in literature. It was obvious by the end of the Quattrocento that vernacular literature was in the ascendant, and not in Italy alone but in other Western European countries, even in Germany where humanist influence was particularly powerful. It is hardly surprising that the four most influential writers of Renaissance Italy—Sannazzaro, Castiglione, Ariosto, and Machiavelli—chose to write their masterpieces in Italian. What is surprising is that their influence was, for different reasons in each case, as overwhelming abroad as at home, and surpassed only by the influence of the love poems of Petrarch and the *Decameron* of Boccaccio. North of the Alps, these writers were the teachers of sixteenth-century Europe. That their chief works were in Italian and not in the internationally understood Latin was not really an obstacle. With foreign students flocking to the universities of Italy, with English, French, Spanish, and German travellers visiting the country, Italian quickly became the best-known foreign language, just as French had been in the Middle Ages and was to be again from the seventeenth century until a generation ago.

The appeal of these writers, as far as three of them were

concerned, was that they supplied dazzling pictures of idealized worlds, unreal yet not so distant from reality as, for instance, the world of *Gulliver's Travels*. It was, rather, an idealized reality, embodying the yearnings of Renaissance men, and drawing on the fullest resources of humanist culture. The shepherds of Sannazzaro and the knights of Ariosto were no more removed in time from their readers than the courtly society of Castiglione was in space. These shepherds, knights, and courtiers were living Renaissance characters, yet idealized and endowed with the very qualities which most men wished they themselves possessed. As for Machiavelli, his appeal rested on the general belief that his was the way to political success. If the means he advocated were often repugnant, their success was preferable to a morality which could only be its own reward.

Apart from Machiavelli, each of the writers considered in this chapter was a humanist. Sannazzaro composed Latin lyrics and a notable large-scale Christian epic in Virgilian hexameters, the *De partu Virginis*, which was still being read in theological colleges on the Continent as recently as last century. He also made a search for ancient texts when in France in 1501-4, and was rewarded by the discovery of some forgotten classical poems. Castiglione also wrote in Latin. While in Rome he became interested in archaeology, and was the actual author of Raphael's report to Pope Leo X on the antiquities of the eternal city. The humanist activity of Ariosto, less of a scholar than the two others, did not go much beyond writing Latin lyrics and reading ancient poets more for pleasure than for real study, more in order to capture vague echoes of antiquity than for precise information. On the whole, theirs was a literary humanism; not so with Machiavelli, whose approach to the classics was that of a historian rather than a humanist.

Machiavelli had no Greek, and was forced to rely on Latin versions in order to read the Greek historians. But his chief interest was in the Roman historians. These he read, not for stylistic beauties, or rare words or choice turns of phrase, but for the facts which would lend authority to his own theories. Though not a humanist, he adopts a humanist point of view, seeing the ideal form of government as that of Republican Rome.

Sannazzaro, Castiglione and Ariosto, unlike Machiavelli, were not born or brought up in Tuscany. They typify an Italy which had accepted Tuscan as the language of literature, but which was now busy surpassing the Tuscans themselves. It was their contemporary, Pietro Bembo (1470–1547), a Venetian, who was recognized as the supreme authority on all questions relating to Tuscan literary usage. Again, the first Italian grammar to appear in print (in 1516) was the work of Gianfrancesco Fortunio, who was a northerner.

Jacopo Sannazzaro was born in 1455 or 1456 and was brought up in Naples at a time when the Aragonese rulers of this city had to contend with an invasion by an Angevin pretender as well as frequent baronial rebellions, which they suppressed ruthlessly. A poet within the humanist tradition, Sannazzaro had turned to Petrarch for his Italian poetry, and to Virgil and the elegiac poets for his Latin poetry. His vernacular writings, such as the farces and the *Gliommeri*, merely reflect the influence of courtly and popular literature and show a ready facility for versification. Had Sannazzaro written nothing else, he would be completely forgotten. What assured him an important place in literature was his *Arcadia*, composed about 1480–5.

The first version of the *Arcadia* was written in a language which tried to imitate that of the great Florentine writers and particularly of Boccaccio. It was a hybrid language, however, and Sannazzaro was acutely aware of this. Accordingly, the work was thoroughly revised, and in 1504 a final text appeared, from which most of the non-Tuscan features had been eradicated. The *Arcadia* immediately proved a great success. A modern reader is likely to find it monotonous and even slightly ridiculous, but the style of the *Arcadia*, with its involved latinizing sentences and extravagant imagery, greatly appealed to an age dominated by classicism.

Dante's *Vita Nuova* and Boccaccio's *Fiammetta* had inaugurated a fashion for autobiographical romances. There was, in addition, a strong surviving tradition of pastoral poetry fostered by Virgil and other Latin writers of eclogues, which had survived the Middle Ages. Dante, Petrarch, Boccaccio, and countless humanists after them had written Latin eclogues; Leon Battista Alberti had written at least one eclogue in vernacular, while Sannazzaro himself removed the scene of the eclogues from the fields to the sea in his *Eclogae piscatoriae*. In his *Ninfale Fiesolano* Boccaccio had given poetic life to the landscape around Fiesole and peopled it with nymphs; the pastoral element is just as powerful in his *Ameto*, a prose romance with frequent verse passages in the metre employed by Dante in the *Divine Comedy*.

Like Boccaccio's *Ameto*, Sannazzaro's *Arcadia* included both prose and verse. It claimed to be autobiographical and placed its action in the unreal pastoral world of the eclogue. The action was set in Arcadia; not the actual region of Greece, which the author had never visited, but rather the idealized Arcadia of classical poetry. Here, in this enchanted land, Sannazzaro imagines himself, under the name of Sincero, living among the shepherds. He has come to them because of an unhappy love affair, and, like the shepherds, he delights in telling his sorrows and his passionate love for an unresponsive lady to the woods, mountains, and caves. The shepherds are no uncouth rustics, but Renaissance gentlemen, little different from the poet in upbringing and outlook. In fact, when reading the *Arcadia* one gets the impression that every shepherd is really Sannazzaro himself. On the other hand, the setting could scarcely be less like Aragonese Naples. We are shown a country still in a golden age, still unaffected by the struggles and miseries of life, indeed an ideal place for a fifteenth-century humanist, however dull it may seem to us.

The influence of the *Arcadia* proved immense, and it set the pattern for the Renaissance pastoral romance. Politian's *Orfeo* may have been the more brilliant work, but it was from the *Arcadia* that the genre developed. For one thing, it was conceived on broader lines than Politian's play; for another, most of it was in prose. Had the *Arcadia* been exclusively in verse, it is doubtful whether it would have enjoyed greater popularity than Boccaccio's *Ninfale Fiesolano*, in an age when long narrative poems were expected to be full of blood and thunder, not the musings of a love-sick poet.

Sannazzaro created a mythical pastoral country. Baldesar Castiglione created a court not much less mythical and a concept of courtliness with no counterpart in Renaissance practice. The miseries of court life had been a favourite theme in medieval and Renaissance literature. Dante had exposed them in a few poignant lines of the *Inferno*; and the theme of the 'miseria curialium' attracted, among others, Aeneas Sylvius Piccolomini, the gifted humanist who became Pope Pius II (1458–64). It remained for Ariosto's *Satire* to paint a sordid but convincing picture of court life in all its pettiness. Castiglione himself was not without personal experience of courts. Born in 1478, he had been brought up in Milan, where he received most of his education at the ducal court. Here Ludovico Maria Sforza had finally secured the throne for himself in 1494 by disposing of his nephew and ward, Duke Giovanni Galeazzo. He had earlier removed his nephew's most influential supporters, and was clearly the kind of man who did not object to crime if it was to his advantage. Yet, despite this, his court was the most brilliant of its time in Italy, and some of the greatest artists of the age—Leonardo da Vinci, for instance—were happy to work there. Ludovico's final downfall in 1500 at the hands of the French was the result, not of his crimes, but of his lack of sound political judgement, a deficiency made all the more dangerous by his high opinion of his own mastery of statecraft.

The dubious morality of the Sforza court does not seem to have concerned Castiglione. After leaving it he was for some time employed by his own lord, the ruler of Mantua, and eventually entered the service of Guidobaldo da Montefeltro, Duke of Urbino. The father of Guidobaldo, Duke Federigo, had been a condottiere with a genuine enthusiasm for art and letters and an unusual reputation for honesty. Though it was under his command that the Florentines perpetrated the outrageous sack of Volterra in 1472, he was generally regarded as a good and just man, as well as an accomplished soldier and astute statesman. Guidobaldo sought to resemble his father, but was prevented by poor health from imitating his exploits in the field, and by a limited imagination from equalling him as a patron of art and letters.

When Castiglione reached Urbino, Guidobaldo had only recently recovered the dukedom from which he had been violently ejected by Caesar Borgia. His wife, Elisabetta Gonzaga, had shown herself to be an intellectual, and her husband's court was at that time the residence of some remarkable men. In 1507, the year in which the dialogues of Castiglione are set, there lived at Urbino Pietro Bembo, then recognized as the arbiter on all questions of literary taste, and an authority on the Platonic theory of love. There too was Bibbiena, who later became a cardinal. There were also prominent political refugees, such as Giuliano de Medici the Younger, and the Fregoso brothers, Federico and Ottaviano. Altogether it was a brilliant company, rich in humanist learning and at the same time sparkling with wit and intelligence.

During the March evenings of 1507 discussions at court turned much on the qualities of the perfect courtier, and Castiglione took full note of them. Then, in 1508, Guidobaldo died childless. Castiglione, after spending some time in the service of his successor, the despicable Francesco Maria della Rovere, entered the papal diplomatic service, became a bishop and the Pope's nuncio in Madrid, and finally died there in 1528. What interests us here is not Castiglione the diplomat, but the man whom Emperor Charles V described as 'the best of all knights'. Although the *Cortegiano* portrays an idealized courtier, there is no doubt that it expressed Castiglione's own views on courtly behaviour.

The *Libro del Cortegiano* openly claimed to reflect the Urbino conversations of 1507. How accurately its dialogues do in fact reproduce these conversations is a matter of speculation. Castiglione certainly gave them unity and literary shape, and in this he was much influenced by Cicero's *De Officiis*. What, then, were the qualities necessary to the courtier? The first dialogue provides the obvious answer: noble birth, proficiency in arms, and the knightly virtues. But the requirements went further. The courtier must not be an uncouth boor, as some Renaissance princes were, but must have a taste for letters and the arts. Manners were of paramount importance, and here the *Cortegiano* provides us with the courtly counterpart of Della Casa's *Galateo*, which set up standards for anyone of the middle class aspiring to polished manners. Wit was another essential for the courtier, and in this a lead was given by Bibbiena with his dissertation on 'Facetiae', those popular anecdotes which would hardly be tolerated now in polite society. The female counterpart of the courtier is also discussed. Needless to say, she is not called 'cortegiana' (which means 'courtesan'), but 'donna di palazzo', the 'palace lady', whose idealized portrait is drawn by Giuliano de Medici.

There remained one important question, the relationship between prince and courtier. This could at times be highly complex, and unwise opposition to the ruler might lead to immediate dismissal. Ottaviano Fregoso dealt with this aspect, although one is left wondering how much his sensible views were actually followed in practice. The *Cortegiano* ends with a disquisition on Platonic love, a topic strangely popular with the courtly company, which could listen unblushingly to the coarsest stories or the most obscene comedies. The spokesman here was Pietro Bembo, whose views had their ultimate source in Marsilio Ficino.

The *Cortegiano*, then, presents us again with an idealized view of reality. But whereas that evoked by Sannazzaro depicted a scene utterly remote from his readers, Castiglione chose to place before his contemporaries their own world not as it was but as one might have desired it to be. What he offered to courtiers was a model of behaviour which it was within their power to achieve. Had Castiglione written with the outlook of a Machiavelli, his courtier and his palace lady would have been different beings. Their ideals and their graceful manners would have been replaced by jealousy, sordid motives, and a mania for 'getting on'. Instead, the *Cortegiano* came to represent the European ideal of courtliness, while the author became a living symbol of all that was best in a gentleman. This fundamentally humanist ideal was founded on the sense of proportion which had been the secret of Vittorino da Feltre's success as an educator. The same virtue had characterized Duke Federigo himself, Guidobaldo's father, whose example must have conditioned the conversations held in March 1507 in the Urbino palace he had built.

The *Cortegiano* thus has its foundations rooted in reality. Ariosto, on the other hand, like Sannazzaro preferred to seek refuge in a fictitious world. The *Orlando Furioso* reveals this imaginative side, which is more representative of Ariosto than his *Satire*, with its portrayal of the miseries and petty squalors of everyday life. Ariosto, like Castiglione, had been brought up in a courtly atmosphere. Born at Reggio Emilia in 1474, he moved at the age of ten to Ferrara, a town which then seemed to him the most desirable place on earth and remained so to the end of his life. He had been unfortunate, to say the least, in the choice of his father. For messer Niccolò Ariosto, a high official of the Duke of Ferrara, was one of the dreaded instruments of the Este tyranny, not above accepting bribes, and cordially disliked by the Duke's subjects. At that time in Italy, as now, legal studies were considered the best avenue to a successful career. Ariosto, despite his loathing for jurisprudence, was thus forced by his father to read civil law. It was only after he had wasted five years in this study that he was finally allowed to have his own way and devote himself to the humanities. Ferrara was still reaping the benefits of the teaching of Guarino da Verona, who, from 1429 until his death at the age of ninety in 1460, had made the University the leading school of humanities in Europe. Ariosto felt this influence powerfully during his formative years. Latin versification was his earliest literary activity; indeed when he was twenty (despite what he says in his satire to Bembo, that at that age he hardly had any Latin) he produced a Latin sapphic ode 'Ad Philiroem', which was occasioned by Charles VIII's entry into Italy.

What really turned Ariosto into an accomplished scholar, however, was his brief contact with the humanist teacher Gregorio da Spoleto. This influence upon him was timely, since from 1502 onwards he was no longer his own master. First, he was put in charge of the castle of Canossa, the place where in 1077 the Emperor Henry IV had thrown himself at the feet of Pope Gregory VII. Then from 1503 onwards he was in the employment of Cardinal Ippolito d'Este. It was while in the Cardinal's service that he composed the first classical comedy in Italian, the *Cassaria*, and this was followed by another, also modelled on Plautus and Terence, *I Suppositi*. It was also during this period that he wrote his masterpiece the *Orlando Furioso*, first printed at Ferrara in 1516.

Ariosto expected great things from this poem. But his master looked on Ariosto as a courtier, whose duty it was to devote himself to the Cardinal's business and undertake a series of missions. In short, Ariosto and the Cardinal had widely differing conceptions of a courtier's duties, and the most surprising thing about their parting in 1517 is that it had not happened long before. As far as his dealings with the Cardinal are concerned we possess, of course, only Ariosto's version. Doubtless the Cardinal, whose behaviour towards his wretched half-brother Don Giulio did him no credit, was an exacting taskmaster; none the less, Ariosto was able to write the *Orlando Furioso* while in his employment.

After leaving the Cardinal, Ariosto entered the service of his elder brother Duke Alfonso, now mainly remembered as the third and last husband of Lucretia Borgia and a leading expert in efficient gunnery. This appointment involved three years (1522–5) among the cut-throats of the Garfagnana, trying to establish law and order without either the necessary means or the essential backing of the Duke. But at last in 1525 Ariosto was again in Ferrara, where the revision of the *Orlando Furioso* kept him busy for the rest of his life.

The culture of late-fifteenth-century Ferrara was twofold. Classicism had been established there, mainly through the efforts of Guarino. But among the upper nobility, from the Duke downwards, French romances were even more popular than the classics. In a way, Boiardo had reflected both these sides of Ferrarese culture, and in the *Orlando Innamorato* had presented the old epic matter tempered by the refinement of the Arthurian romances and the sophistication of humanism. The French invasion of 1494 and the death of Boiardo ended the poem abruptly. The aim of Ariosto was to continue the *Orlando Innamorato*, but in a spirit of complete freedom. Boiardo's poem, though animated by Renaissance culture, still retained a certain Gothic stiffness. This was not so with the *Orlando Furioso*, which differed as much from its predecessor as a picture by one of the Ferrarese Quattrocento masters, say Cossa or Tura, differs from a Giorgione or a Titian.

Deriving its title from Seneca's *Hercules Furens*, the *Orlando Furioso* draws much upon the *Aeneid* and the *Iliad*. The poem opens with the Moors laying siege to Paris after defeating Charlemagne in battle. But though this war was a holy one, with Christianity on the defensive against Islam, it is not the most important element in the poem. It merely serves as a framework, like the plague in the *Decameron*, and what really matters is the succession of episodes within it. Of these, the two chief concern the madness of Orlando, which is reminiscent of the wrath of Achilles in the *Iliad*, and the adventures of Ruggiero, the Saracen. Ariosto has little use for Charlemagne, whom the earlier *Cantari* had already turned, as we have seen, into the 're Carlone', a figure of fun and a synonym for clumsiness. It is the heroes and their amorous adventures that stimulate his poetic imagination most effectively. What Ariosto describes is an enchanted world, remote from the grim realities of early-sixteenth-century Italy, when the armies of France and Spain were busy turning the Peninsula into a battlefield. It was Ariosto's ability to create a world in which the dreams of Renaissance men found poetic reality that made the *Orlando Furioso* a masterpiece in a way that *Italia Liberata dai Goti* or *Amadigi* or the countless other poems that followed in its wake certainly were not. But what also made the *Orlando Furioso* unique was its musical diction and dazzling imagery. The *Orlando Furioso* was the supreme poetic expression of the Renaissance, just as Tasso's *Gerusalemme Liberata* was of the age of the Counter-Reformation.

Ariosto and Castiglione, and, to a lesser extent, Sannazzaro, were typical products of Renaissance courtliness. It was quite a different story with Machiavelli. Both by birth and upbringing a Florentine, he too had lived in an Italy subject to foreign invasions and in a Florence where the power and influence of the Medici saw periods of ascendancy and decline. He had witnessed the rise and fall of Savonarola, and had learnt from it that only armed prophets can succeed. He had seen the horrors of Borgia rule and appreciated the realities of French and Spanish power. Born in 1469, he had read the Latin classics, but in the city of Politian and the Platonic Academy he had failed to learn Greek, and knew Greek writers only in Latin translations.

The literary career of Machiavelli was the logical conclusion of his public career. For from 1498, when he secured employment in the Florentine chancery, until the return of the Medici in 1512, he was in the very centre of affairs. What fascinated him most were the realities of political power, and he did not lack material for his observation. His experience with the Florentine troops at the siege of Pisa gave him an insight into the true nature of armies; he learnt from a mission to France that a centralized monarchy was the real source of French power, and from a further mission to Germany that the autonomy of German towns was the cause of their prosperity. But the most formative of his missions were the two he undertook to Caesar Borgia in 1502. Caesar's inhuman deeds were observed not with the eyes of a moralist but with the detachment of one anxious to unravel their political lesson. Thus, when Caesar treacherously captured and put to death a group of condottieri scarcely better than himself, Machiavelli analysed the deed from a purely political angle; and politically it could meet only with his approval. This does not mean that he was a cold-blooded cynic. He was a good citizen, a warm friend, a devoted father, a patriot, even an idealist. His idealism, however, was vitiated by a lack of faith in men, which was echoed in his bitter acknowledgement that the views he held would have been abominable if men were not evil. But they were evil, and Frenchmen, Italians, and Spaniards were the scum of the earth. Infinitely preferable were the mountaineers of Germany, whom he regarded in the same light as Tacitus had regarded the German tribesmen of his time, some seventeen hundred years before Rousseau discovered his 'noble savage'. Machiavelli abominated mercenaries, whose unreliability he had witnessed again and again, and in their place envisaged a town militia. He did not recognize that such a militia would have no chance against the well-drilled infantries of Louis XII and Ferdinand the Catholic.

The return of the Medici to Florence in 1512 meant the end of Machiavelli as a public servant. Banished to San

Casciano, a few miles away, he employed his enforced leisure in theorizing from his political and diplomatic experience. He had by then made his most important discovery, the autonomy of politics. Hitherto theorists had treated politics as a branch of moral philosophy, though this was certainly not reflected by current practice. He profoundly disagreed with this approach, and meditated on the writings of the ancient historians in order to find confirmation for his views. What really mattered most to him was to find a valid formula for the preservation and prosperity of the state, and on this he concentrated his speculations. He embarked upon a series of short dissertations based on Livy's first decade, the *Discorsi*, in which he considered the ideal form of state; that is to say, the republic. The government of republics, their territorial expansion, the conditions essential to their stability, the sources of their strength, the causes of their decay, these were the main objects of his investigations, which he conducted with a logic, depth, and objectivity worthy of Aristotle. His conclusions were sometimes startling. Though a staunch republican, he admitted also that a state could be founded and ordained only by an absolute ruler. He maintained again and again that political science had one supreme and ultimate aim, the preservation of the state, and no course of action that could prevent its ruin was to be regarded as wicked. And what of religion? Machiavelli saw it as a potential instrument of policy, and he openly preferred the religion of the ancient Romans to Christianity because of its emphasis on patriotism.

The best known of Machiavelli's works, the one which made him both famous and infamous, a Protestant in the eyes of Catholics and a disguised 'Jesuit' in the eyes of Protestants, was not the *Discorsi* but the *Principe*. Started after the *Discorsi*, it was completed before it in 1513. It was in fact an offshoot of the major work, an offshoot which was itself a short set of variations on the theme of monarchy. In a way it was an occasional work, prompted by a desire to curry favour with the new Medici rulers and particularly with Giuliano the Younger (the member of the family who figures so prominently in Castiglione's *Cortegiano*). The particular doctrines advocated in it were drawn mainly from the practice of fifteenth-century princes like King Ferrante I, Francesco Sforza, Caesar Borgia, Ferdinand the Catholic, and Louis XI. Since the main aim of Machiavelli's ruler was to be successful, nothing was to be allowed to stand in his way. Yet in the last chapter of the book there is a sudden change. The dispassionate tone becomes now highly emotional, and the *Principe* ends quite unexpectedly with a peroration advocating, with all the warmth and eloquence which could be marshalled by the writer, the unification of Italy under a single prince.

Machiavelli's other works included comedies—one of which, the *Mandragola*, is outstanding—as well as political tracts, poems, and dialogues on the art of war. His *Storie Fiorentine*, dedicated to Pope Clement VII and published with his support, yet placed on the papal index by Pope Paul IV, inaugurated modern historiography. In this book, which ends with the death of Lorenzo the Magnificent in 1492, he not only revealed the political lessons of historical events but sought confirmation in them for his own theories. Unlike the historians who preceded him, he emphasized the link between an event and what followed it, and excluded Providence altogether as a determining factor in human affairs. Man, and man alone, he believed was what mattered in history.

These four writers, then, were the leaders of the European literary Renaissance, and no Western European country failed to feel their influence. Their main works were read both in the original and in translation, and determined to some degree the complexion and outlook of Western European literature of the time. Just as Ambrose, Augustine, Gregory, and Jerome were the four doctors of the Latin Church, so Sannazzaro, Castiglione, Ariosto, and Machiavelli were the four secular doctors of Renaissance letters.

# 7

# Italian humanism in Western Europe

THE Italian humanists of the fifteenth century did not limit
themselves to securing a better understanding of the Latin
and Greek classics, but ensured that their newly won learning affected every branch of knowledge. From theology to
law, from medicine to mathematics, no discipline remained
untouched. But humanist influence went beyond the sphere
of learned activities. It also coloured the way of life of
fifteenth-century Italy; it led to a conception of the dignity
of man which had long been forgotten, to a view of
'vita civile' in which man was the most important being.
Fifteenth-century Italy thus differed widely from the rest of
Western Europe. Little wonder, then, that the students who
resorted to Italy to study under the great humanist masters
came to feel like those Roman contemporaries of Cicero
who went to pursue their studies in Athens. Italy was
regarded as the home of all eloquence; to study at an
Italian university became the ambition of every young man
with a bent for rhetoric, law, or medicine.

Italian humanism eventually took root abroad. Already
in Petrarch's time his intellectual outlook had affected some
of his foreign friends and devotees—the imperial chancellor,
Johann von Neumarkt, for instance. In France during the
later decades of the fourteenth and the early decades of the
fifteenth centuries there were scholars like Gontier Col,
Jean de Montreuil, and Nicholas de Clemanges who
modelled their activity upon Petrarch. This early French
humanism did not survive the desolation of the great schism

and the horrors of the later stages of the Hundred Years War. When humanism revived in France other countries were also busy experimenting with it. By the beginning of the sixteenth century there were scholars north of the Alps who were certainly not behind their colleagues from Italy. In fact, Erasmus, Budé, and Thomas More had no equals in Italy.

A powerful propagating factor in the spreading of humanism was the Papacy. As an international institution it had its officials all over Western Christendom. Legates, nuncios, collectors of Peter's Pence, went everywhere, and the majority of these officials had received a humanist education, had humanist tastes, and were often themselves professed humanists. While residing abroad, these men continued to cultivate their studies and in this way influenced the ecclesiastics and laymen with whom they came into contact. At the same time there were the many clerks who came to the court of Rome on business and often remained for some considerable time; there were non-Italian churchmen who became regular curial officials and usually returned home only when appointed to a bishopric or deanery; and there were the foreign students, who attended Italian universities to study medicine, theology, or law, and came under the influence of humanist rhetoric. Finally, we must not forget the Italian humanists who went abroad to earn a living as teachers of rhetoric or as secretaries. These scholars had experienced difficulty in finding employment in Italy, not being men of exceptional ability, but abroad they met with appreciation and contributed powerfully to the acceptance and consolidation of humanism in Western Europe.

Local circumstances moulded the character of humanism in each country. Even in Italy, Venetian humanism had differed from Milanese. Florentine, Roman, and Neapolitan humanism, all displayed distinctive features. We need not be surprised, then, that in Castile humanism assumed both a courtly and a theological complexion, with a particular emphasis on biblical studies. In Germany it was adopted by some theologians, but it also acquired a markedly antiquarian bias. It was Valla, Politian, and Ermolao Barbaro who became the humanist teachers of Europe, but the successor to Politian's *Miscellanea* was Budé's *De Asse*, the work of a non-Italian scholar.

In France Petrarch's example had found imitators but, as I have said, these early French humanist efforts were not long-lived. A thorough investigation of humanism in France between 1420 and 1460, which still remains to be carried out, might reveal evidence that humanist activity took place during these decades. According to present knowledge there was a lull until the arrival in Paris in 1456 of Gregorio da Città di Castello or Tifernate to teach rhetoric. This time humanism had come to stay. Gregorio's lectures on the classics were attended by crowds of enthusiastic students, whose main concern was the improvement of their Latin. In a university torn by struggles between nominalists and realists Robert Gaguin and Guillaume Fichet preferred to turn their attention to the humanities. So when the first book was printed in Paris it was not a theological treatise or a law handbook but the formulary of Latin letters by Gasparino Barzizza. Gaguin and his friends soon became the centre of the Paris humanist world. Needless to say, theirs was an entirely Latin humanism, which concentrated on rhetoric with particular emphasis on versification, oratory, and letter-writing. For a time, lectures were given in Paris by a group including Filippo Beroaldo (who also lectured at Lyons), Fausto Andrelini, Girolamo Balbi, and Cornelio Vitelli. But the humanist quarrels which were so frequent in Italy now broke out also in France, and eventually Andrelini was the only Italian humanist teaching in Paris. Andrelini spent the rest of his life in France, where he alternated the teaching of the Latin classics with the composing of occasional verse under the patronage first of Charles VIII and then of Louis XII. As a lecturer, he was extremely successful, but his effective contribution to the development of humanism in France was not great. What was really needed was a teacher of Greek, and for this Paris had to wait until

1476, when the Byzantine refugee George Hermonymos settled there as a teacher and scribe. As a teacher, Hermonymos did not prove particularly inspiring, but he had his importance, since it was under him that Budé learnt the rudiments of the language. Another Greek, John Lascaris, who followed Hermonymos, was a quite different type of scholar, deriving from the Florence of Lorenzo de Medici and Marsilio Ficino. With teachers like Lascaris and Aleandro, Greek studies developed quickly and made an important contribution to French humanism.

By the early sixteenth century this humanism had drawn strength from several sources, and even some of the schoolmen became involved in it. Pico della Mirandola's humanist philosophy found many followers, and humanist texts were in great demand, particularly those printed by Ascentius Badius. A typical example of the impact of humanism upon a schoolman may be seen in Jacques Lefèvre d'Étaples (1450–1537), whose intellectual interests even extended to oriental languages. Indeed Lefèvre was really a French Pico, though his leaning towards mysticism did not divert him from moral philosophy, music, and the editing of classical and sacred texts. Yet he still believed in the authenticity of Seneca's correspondence with St. Paul, two generations after Valla had established its spuriousness. France was in some ways well behind Italy in the humanist field. The one exception was Guillaume Budé (1468–1540), who in his day had no one to match him as scholar, whether in Italy or elsewhere. In his *De Asse* and *Adnotationes Pandectales* he showed an insight, a range of critical power, and a command of the relevant literature such as Italy had not seen since the deaths of Politian and Ermolao Barbaro. Beside him the other French scholars were dwarfs. Yet one cannot claim him as a typical product of French humanism. He did not represent that merging of traditions which was the outstanding achievement of such as Lefèvre d'Étaples or Charles de Bouelles, and which contributed so much to the moulding of the young Erasmus.

The cradle of French humanism was the University of Paris: that of English humanism was the household of Humfrey, Duke of Gloucester. Had Jean, Duke of Berry —to whom we owe those delightful Books of Hours—lived a generation later, he might have done for France what Duke Humfrey did for England. Before Duke Humfrey's time English intellectuals were too immature to derive any real profit from their occasional contacts with Italian humanism. Even Poggio, one of the greatest humanists of his time, who was in England from 1418 to 1422, had no lasting influence. No wonder, then, that the Duke was particularly anxious to do something about it.

It is not quite clear what made him first turn to the Italians. Probably his meetings with the papal collector of Peter's Pence, Piero del Monte, who was in England from 1434 to 1440, had something to do with it. For Del Monte happened to be an accomplished humanist, and we know that during his frequent meetings with Duke Humfrey he talked to him frequently about the humanist world of Italy and provided him with selected books by the leading humanists of the day.

Del Monte also saw to it that Duke Humfrey employed some Italian humanists as secretaries in his household. Furthermore, since the Duke was much interested in politics and anxious to read the *Republic* of Plato in a worthy Latin version, Del Monte made it possible for him to have this work specially translated by a leading Italian humanist. In the meantime Humfrey's Italian secretary, Tito Livio Frulovisi, composed for his employer a Latin life of King Henry V, which was really a political manifesto in humanist style, advocating the continuation of the war against Burgundy. The Flanders expedition of 1436 prompted Frulovisi to write the *Humfroidos*, a panegyric in Latin verse of the Duke's deeds in the Low Countries after England had broken with Philip the Good, Duke of Burgundy. Frulovisi's successor, Antonio Beccaria of Verona, concentrated his efforts upon translating into Latin the Greek writings of St.

Athanasius, which the Duke was particularly anxious to read, not only on account of their orthodoxy but also because he felt that they might provide useful ammunition against the Lollards. Humfrey was naturally an enthusiastic bibliophile, and his library included a large proportion of humanist volumes imported from Italy. It seems at first sight surprising that he was prepared to part with so many of them during his lifetime; but there was method behind his donations of books in 1439–44 to the Oxford Library which still bears his name. For his intention was to improve the general state of learning, and in particular the standards of Latin writing in the University.

This action had the effect he hoped for. It was partly, if not entirely, due to its influence that certain Oxford scholars decided to study the humanities in Italy. It is true that William Grey, later Bishop of Ely from 1454 to 1478, went to Italy, like so many others, because he was prevented by the war from going to study in Paris. What is more, Grey, and after him Robert Flemmyng, went primarily to study theology. But, once in Italy, they succumbed to the lure of humanism and, after securing their degrees at Padua, they moved to Ferrara in order to attend the classes of Guarino da Verona. These same classes were later attended also by John Free, John Gunthorpe, and John Tiptoft, Earl of Worcester. By their day, however, men were drawn to Italy mostly by a wish to improve their grasp of the humanities. Not that their approach to the humanities was identical in every case. Grey and Tiptoft were great nobles; it was natural that patronage and book-collecting should be their principal interests. Gunthorpe and Flemmyng were churchmen; their aim was to achieve proficiency in humanist letters, though in fact they never came near to Italian professional standards. It remained for John Free to become the first Englishman whose Latin was indistinguishable from that of the best Italian humanists and whose Greek was certainly not inferior to theirs.

John Free never returned home, but died in Italy in 1465.

The other English pupils of Guarino returned to England and by their patronage and example gave new strength to the rising tide of humanism. Further stimulus came from visits of Italian humanist teachers. Stefano Surigone, who lectured at Oxford in the 1460s, was instrumental in starting William Sellyng on the humanist path, and Sellyng became in due course a very influential scholar. Later in the century, Lorenzo da Savona and Caio Auberino at Cambridge, and Cornelio Vitelli at Oxford, proved highly successful teachers.

It was a sign of the changing intellectual climate that George Neville, Archbishop of York (d. 1476), should himself be interested in Greek, even to the extent of taking Greek scholars into his employ. This, as well as the steadily increasing flow of humanist manuals from Italy into England, made it possible for humanism here to reach its maturity by the end of the century. The leading exponents then were William Grocin, John Colet, and Thomas Linacre, all of whom had received part of their education in Italy. As it happened, Sir Thomas More (1480–1535) became the greatest of all English humanists, though he had never studied abroad; yet even he was not altogether free from Italian influence, particularly that of Pico della Mirandola, an author who also proved very congenial to Colet.

Most of the great English humanists of the early sixteenth century—even More, the layman—were deeply interested in theology. The circle of court humanists, however, where Cornelio Vitelli, Pietro Carmeliano, and Giovanni Gigli held sway, was dominated by a rhetorical approach and revealed a distinct taste for Latin versification.

In the Low Countries humanism had a decidedly religious character, springing as it did from the efforts of the Brethren of the Common Life. This religious society of laymen became famous for its educational activities. Its schools, of which the one of Alexander Hegius at Deventer was the most famous, sought to combine the traditional grammatical teaching of the Middle Ages with study of the leading humanist manuals from Italy. Alexander of Villedieu was read side by side with Valla and Perotti. A product of these schools was Rudolf Agricola (1444–1485), who quickly assimilated humanist rhetoric and humanist methods and became an outstanding scholar in his country. From them, too, came John Wessel of Gansfort (d. 1489); his contacts with Italy, however, did not turn him from his biblical studies nor shake his allegiance to William of Ockham, but strengthened a burning zeal for religious reform long before the days of Luther. Finally, it was from Hegius at Deventer that Erasmus received his schooling.

Erasmus (1467–1536) does not belong to the humanism of the Netherlands. He belongs to European humanism. In him are blended the teaching of the Brethren of the Common Life, the scholastic humanism of late-fifteenth-century Paris, the critical methods of Valla, and the hellenism of Aldus's Venetian Academy. In his editing of the Fathers, in his semi-philosophical handbooks, in his *Adagia*, in his *Praise of Folly*, and in his countless letters, he showed himself independent of every school and group. He had succeeded in assimilating and harmonizing all the various intellectual streams of his day. His humanist ideals were, above all, Christian ideals. Nevertheless, he adhered neither to Pope Leo X nor to Martin Luther; his beliefs came closest to Colet's, in the more articulate form in which they were expressed by Sir Thomas More. Thus he represented the highest aspirations of a Europe torn between Catholics and Reformers—a Europe which was losing the spiritual unity it had enjoyed for a thousand years.

In comparison with Erasmus, the Flemish humanist Christopher de Longueil, commonly known as Longolius (1488–1522), was a dim figure, though his violent Ciceronianism made some impression in Italy, where he spent the last years of his brief life. In Louvain University humanism made little headway during the first two decades of the sixteenth century, except in such fields as grammar and rhetoric. Certainly the Louvain vice-chancellor, Hadrian

Florents of Utrecht, who ruled the Church as Pope Hadrian VI (1521–3), was no humanist.

The situation was very different in Germany; that is to say, in the area including not only the imperial domains as they stood at the death of Maximilian I in 1519 but also a good deal of Switzerland. German humanism originated in the universities at Erfurt, Heidelberg, Leipzig, Basle, and Vienna. Great humanist scholars like Cardinal Nicholas of Cusa (1401–1464) had indeed assimilated their humanism in Italy. But the real pioneers were the Italian scholars at the German universities who taught rhetoric and poetics and lectured on some of the more widely read Latin classics, such as Virgil and Terence. Working with them were noted scholars like Peter Luder of Heidelberg. Such teachers, whether German or Italian, as well as German-born students who habitually resorted to Italian universities, as they had done since the thirteenth century, were together instrumental in securing the acceptance of the new humanistic values.

German humanism at an early stage began to display distinct antiquarian traits. Antiquarian humanists like Hartmann and Hermann Schedel owed their tastes to their years in Italy, where archaeological science had been flourishing since the days of Poggio and Biondo. These in their turn were followed by Peutinger, Celtis, and many others. Despite the loose political unity that prevailed under the Emperor Maximilian I, the feeling of being a German, of belonging to 'Germania', became particularly marked. German humanists began to sigh after a German past which was in their view just as great as, perhaps greater than, the Roman one. In particular, Conrad Celtis (1459–1508) directed his efforts towards reminding his fellow Germans of their remote ancestors. He rescued from oblivion forgotten texts in medieval Latin, which showed that the Germans had not been quite inarticulate during the Middle Ages. His editing of Hroswitha's plays and of the *Ligurinus* of Gunther the Cistercian was a conscious reply to the humanist editing of classical texts. Moreover, just as

Biondo had written an *Italia illustrata,* so now Celtis produced a *Germania illustrata.* Again, like the Italians the Germans began to collect the ancient inscriptions of their country. Here Peutinger led the way with a collection of Roman inscriptions to be found in the *Ager Moguntinum,* an example quickly followed by others. This national feeling became even stronger after Luther had broken with Rome. The German past was now openly set up against the Roman past. Arminius was hailed as the national German hero because he had been the first to show that the Romans were not invincible.

Everywhere the impact of Italian humanism on Western Europe led to the development in each country of a national humanism with special features of its own. Now we have to remember that outside Italy cultural activity was mainly ecclesiastic until the Reformation made possible the rise of a lay culture. In countries untouched by the Reformation the ecclesiastical monopoly of culture went on for some time. This was certainly the case in Spain, but when we talk about Spain we must distinguish between the Castilian and Aragonese domains. Though these had been united since 1479 under Ferdinand and Isabella, they were still divided by language and traditions. During the thirteenth century the patronage of King Alfonso X of Castile (1252–1284), commonly known as El Sabio, 'the wise', had led to the composition of many treatises in Castilian rather than in Latin, and Castilian prose had shown itself capable of the task. By the fifteenth century, however, this tradition of vernacular scholarship, unparalleled in late medieval Europe, had died out and Latin had regained its lost ground. The time was therefore ripe for humanism, and two factors in particular facilitated its acceptance: the intellectual outlook of King John II (1406–1454), and the activity of Alfonso de Santa Maria, Bishop of Burgos, at the Council of Basle, where he made the acquaintance of well-known Italian scholars. Pier Candido Decembrio, one of the leading humanists of the time, kept in touch with both King

95

and Bishop to the extent of submitting to them Latin translations of Greek authors, including some of the books of the *Iliad*.

The introduction of humanist works from Italy into Castile created a taste for such writings and encouraged young men to go to Italian universities to perfect themselves in the humanities. Among them one may note Alfonso Hernández de Palencia, Fernando de Córdoba, and later Antonio de Nebrija. Once in Italy, these scholars modified their original views, broadened their knowledge of the classics, and improved their Latin style beyond recognition. Eventually Fernando de Córdoba switched from the study of the humanities to that of philosophy, and won a great reputation in France and Italy. Alfonso Hernández de Palencia, on the other hand, chose to return home and introduced Italian humanist traditions into the Castilian chancery, where two Italian humanists later succeeded him, first Antonio Geraldini and then Peter Martyr of Anghiera. Finally Nebrija applied his new learning to fields of scholarship ranging from historiography to biblical studies, as well as to Castilian grammar.

Castilian humanism affected both court and universities, and Castilian and Italian humanists lectured at the University of Salamanca. When Cardinal Ximenes founded a university at Alcalá de Henares in 1508 he imported humanists from Salamanca University, among them Nebrija. Ximenes had in mind some ambitious schemes, including the preparation of a new and accurate Latin translation of the whole of Aristotle (such as Ermolao Barbaro had intended). The Cardinal's death in 1517 brought this project to nothing, but he lived long enough to ensure the publication of the Complutensian Polyglot Bible (Complutum was the Latin name of Alcalá) in which the text of Holy Writ was printed in the various biblical languages, Hebrew, Aramaic, Greek, and Latin. As an achievement the Complutensian Bible was unique in its time. It speaks well not only for the vitality of Castilian humanism but also for its deftness in applying humanist methods to sacred learning. Humanism in the Aragonese territories could offer nothing so exceptional even though it had much older traditions.

Aragonese humanism had made a tentative start during the second half of the fourteenth century, when the Aragonese-born great master of the knights of Rhodes, Joan Hernández de Heredia, encouraged the translation of many Greek texts—the lives of Plutarch and part of Thucydides among them—into his own vernacular. After the death of Heredia, and also of King John I of Aragon, who had to some extent shared his humanist tastes, these activities died away. In 1442 the King of Aragon, Alfonso V, who also ruled over Sicily, added Naples to his domains. Furthermore, he settled there, and his Neapolitan court became one of the leading humanist centres in Italy, with Valla, Facio, and Panormita as its brightest stars. Yet not much of its glamour reached Aragon where, with the exception of Joan Margarit i Pau, who became Bishop of Gerona and a cardinal, and wrote historical works modelled on those of Italian humanists, there was little Italian humanist influence outside the sphere of formal rhetorical teaching. Again, certain Portuguese who had studied at Florence under Politian and at Bologna under Beroaldo and Codro Urceo brought some humanist influence to Portugal. But in the main the results of their humanist experiences were not outstanding.

# 8

# Petrarchism outside Italy

DURING the sixteenth century Petrarchism was Italy's principal literary export. As such it was the immediate successor of humanism, and the counterpart of Ciceronianism in vernacular letters. In fact, the reason why Petrarch became the universal model for love poetry and for other kinds of lyric poetry is to be sought in the new outlook fostered by humanism. The resulting new tastes and standards made existing vernacular literature appear old-fashioned. In the imitation of Petrarch men of letters felt a sense of fulfilment, expressing their new-found passion for rhetoric in a preoccupation with finery and ornament. It was an age when all poets, or nearly all, were formalists.

Yet another reason may be given for Petrarch's astonishing popularity: as a writer he was particularly easy to imitate. But although it was fairly simple to match the external form of his lyric, to achieve his essential quality was quite a different matter. The Italians had been writing love poetry in the style of Petrarch ever since his death, yet not one poet in the Peninsula had come near to the master in quality or genius.

The imitation of Petrarch outside Italy led to a mania for conceits, alliteration, word-play, hyperbole, and antithesis. With all this emphasis on outward form, the subject-matter of lyric poetry tended to become more and more futile, originality of theme exceptional, and feelings inflated and artificial. It was a poetry without half-tones, where everything was as intense as it was dull, and where the same clichés occurred again and again. On both sides of the Alps, lyric poetry was thronged with ladies who were indistinguishable in appearance and behaviour, and monotonously referred to as the 'sweet enemy' or the 'fair inhuman one'. Petrarch's Laura acquired sisters throughout Western Europe all as gifted as she and as pitiless towards the suffering poet. They were the product of poetic convention, and all the qualities and features attributed to them do not succeed in making them real. It was an age, none the less, when one would with ease reel off sonnets containing all the ingredients required by prevalent literary fashion.

During the fifteenth century the salient features of Petrarch's lyric poetry had been thus used and abused by the Italians. Very seldom had they come near its mood, but the formal imitations could vary considerably from poet to poet. With men like Giusto dei Conti and Boiardo, Petrarchism never lost the balanced composure of its model, and with Boiardo it sometimes echoed it with a certain elegance and feeling. With Cariteo, Tebaldeo, and Serafino Aquilano, however, the style degenerated into reckless extravagance, with exaggerated conceits and hyperbole. Here was the poetic counterpart of the Latin prose of the elder Beroaldo and Giovanni Battista Pio, and the vernacular prose of Francesco Colonna. These poets were indeed the forerunners of Euphuism and Marinismo, anticipating the tastes and values of the Baroque one hundred years before Seicentismo became the leading fashion in Italian literature.

All in all, Petrarch proved both a blessing and a curse to European literature. But what makes us overlook his harmful effects is his command of the sonnet, the form which Carducci called 'breve e amplissimo carme' and which inspired Boileau to say that one faultless exemplar 'vaut tout un long poème'. It is true that Petrarch's legacy to Europe also included other metres, such as the 'canzone' and 'sestina', not to mention his popularization of Dante's 'terza rima' in the *Trionfi*. Yet, metrically, Petrarchism meant, above all, the sonnet, and it was with sonnets that it flooded European literature. Among the countries affected by Petrarchism, France and Spain were those which proved most responsive. Naturally, the Latin writings of Petrarch had already been circulating in France during their author's lifetime, while the *Trionfi* were certainly not unknown, either there or in Spain, during the fifteenth century. Knowledge of Petrarch's lyrics, on the other hand, reached France somewhat later, at the time when the French invasion had made things Italian particularly fashionable north of the Alps.

Among the Italian Petrarchists of the late fifteenth century, Serafino Aquilano, whose sensuous love lyrics were generally written in the form of the 'strambotto' (often eight-line stanzas with alternate rhymes), won the approval of the French king, Charles VIII. Another warm admirer of Serafino was Jean Lemaire des Belges (1473–1514), and in fact he paid him the compliment of translating some of his verse in his *Trois comptes intitulez de Cupido et de Atropos*. But, despite his humanist attitudes, Lemaire is better considered as the last medieval 'rhétoriqueur' than the first Renaissance poet writing in French. Clément Marot (1496–1544) was the first Frenchman to try his hand at the writing of sonnets. But then Marot had lived in Italy and had some direct experience of its current literature. Moreover, he was closely connected with the italianate court of Francis I. His *Epigrammes amoureuses* derive straight from Serafino's *Strambotti* except that he refused to adopt the 'rima Baciata', i.e. the rhyming couplet, at the end. Marot's sentiments, his feelings, his rhetorical finery, do not differ very much from those of Cariteo, Tebaldeo, or Serafino. He merely happened to be a better poet.

It was Marot, then, who naturalized Petrarchism on French soil. At the same time his contemporary, Melin de Saint-Gelais (1491–1558), not only sought to follow in the path of Serafino but even fancied himself the Serafino of France. Certainly he came closer to him than Marot had been. Although some of his epigrams are merely litera translations of *Strambotti* by Serafino or other Italian Petrarchists, and some even 'borrow' the original rhyme scheme, it is quite remarkable how he made the imagery, conceits, and superficial phraseology of the Italians his own. If his aim was to be the Serafino of France he certainly achieved it, though he never enjoyed the same extraordinary success as his favourite author had had in courtly society.

Maurice Scève (1500–1560) and his followers were also devotees of Serafino, but Scève's real influence is rather to be sought in his introduction of Platonism into French poetry. His influential position may surprise us, considering that he did not move in courtly circles but among the middle-class society of Lyons. But his *Délie* (1545) is the first French collection of lyrics, the first French 'canzoniere' in the manner of Petrarch. It is true that Scève followed Tebaldeo and Serafino just as his predecessors had done, but in him the obvious sensuality of Serafino's lyric was purified by the Platonist approach to love inaugurated by Ficino. Scève's Platonism was not, however, academic like Ficino's, but sophisticated and courtly like Bembo's in his *Asolani,* or subtle and extravagant like Leone Ebreo's in his *Dialoghi.*

With Scève, Bembo began to exert an influence on French literature, particularly through his Platonism. On the other hand, it was as an orthodox Petrarchist that he later came to play an important role in French Petrarchism, standing out against the popular elements which had crept into Petrarchism through Tebaldeo, Cariteo, Serafino, and their associates. 'Without you', Niccolò Franco had written when Bembo died in 1547, 'we would all have become Tebaldeos.' Serafino had discarded sonnets and 'canzoni' in favour of the plebeian 'strambotti'. It was Bembo who gave new strength to Petrarch's own metres. Thus Jacques Peletier du Mans (1517–1582), Du Bellay's teacher, included some fifteen sonnets in his *Œuvres poétiques* (1547) and twelve of these were straightforward translations of Petrarch, not of his fifteenth- or sixteenth-century imitators. Yet it was not Le Peletier who followed up Scève's *Délie,* but Joachim du

Bellay (1522–1560), with whom French Petrarchism assumed distinctive new features.

In 1548, that is to say just three years after the *Délie*, there appeared Du Bellay's *Déffence et illustration de la langue française*, in which the linguistic theories enunciated by Bembo, Speroni, and Muzio—particularly those of Speroni —were applied to French. To call the *Déffence* a treatise on language would be too narrow. It was intended to be nothing less than a manifesto of the new French poetry, an open declaration of war against Marot and his followers and against all they stood for in poetry. It advocated a new conformity with Italian models. And what Du Bellay advocated in theory he demonstrated in practice with his *Olive* (1549). This was a collection consisting mainly of fifty love sonnets with a preface, in which the author declared himself to have imitated Petrarch and Ariosto. In the second edition, which appeared one year later, the preface was omitted, but the number of sonnets had now risen to one hundred and fifteen.

In *Olive* the debt to Petrarch and the followers of Bembo is quite clear. Some of its sonnets are renderings of love speeches in Ariosto's *Orlando Furioso*, while others clearly derive from a very popular Italian poetic anthology, the *Rime di diversi eccellenti autori*. Yet, despite its evident Petrarchism, the poetry of *Olive* strikes a personal note and succeeds in being lively even though it remains artificial. Both artificiality and subtlety are even more evident in Du Bellay's *XIII sonnets de l'honneste amour*, in which he celebrated the supremacy of spiritual love. Here, however, the main influence is no longer Italian. It may instead be traced to Du Bellay's own contemporary, Pontus de Tyard (1521–1605), whose first book of *Erreurs Amoureuses* was published in Lyons in 1549, the same year as *Olive*.

Pontus de Tyard proclaimed himself a disciple of Scève in the preface to the first book of his *Erreurs*. Indeed, he shared Scève's predilection for Platonism to such an extent that he even turned into French the *Dialoghi* of Leone Ebreo (1551).

The passion he celebrates in his lyrics is, needless to say, a Platonic one, expressed in accordance with the doctrines of Leone Ebreo, but with a rhetoric and formal phraseology derived from Serafino and Tebaldeo. None the less, he succeeded in retaining a typically French flavour in his versification, and this was far from usual in Petrarchists.

On the whole, French Petrarchism before Ronsard was inspired not so much by Petrarch as by his late fifteenth-century imitators, meretricious rhetoric and all. With Pierre de Ronsard (1524–1585), on the other hand, Petrarch became the main model, together with Bembo, the man who had striven to bring back Italian Petrarchism to sanity and a sense of proportion. At least twenty-five sonnets in Ronsard's *Amours* (1552) contain passages taken straight from Petrarch, about a dozen betray his close study of Bembo, and one is clearly derived from Ariosto. It is evident that he relied to a much lesser extent than Du Bellay on the *Rime di diversi eccellenti autori*. A poetic genius of the calibre of Ronsard was not, however, dominated by his models. Even when he openly follows Petrarch or Bembo the accent remains unmistakably personal. In the very structure of the sonnet he refused to follow his Italian models closely. Having judged that the Italian metric scheme did not altogether suit the genius of French lyric poetry, he altered it accordingly. In the *Amours*, these modifications in the sonnet form, together with fine mythological erudition and a highly personal style, resulted in a lyric poetry full of a new sense of harmony and of a liveliness which still retains its charm today.

Up to Ronsard the sonnet was the main form employed by the French Petrarchists. We find a change in the *Amours* of Jean Antoine de Baïf (1532–1589), which also appeared in 1552. Whereas in the first book we find thirty-eight sonnets but only four 'canzoni', the second book contains twenty 'canzoni' and only four sonnets. Such a preponderance of 'canzoni' was indeed a novelty. De Baïf's poetry, however, can hardly be compared with that of Ronsard or Du Bellay.

He never succeeded in avoiding a certain heaviness, not even in the 'canzoni', where he showed himself a much better poet than in the sonnets. Some of the sonnets by De Baïf are literal translations from the Italian. He was obviously not insensitive to the influence of Ariosto; yet both his metric and poetic outlook belong clearly to the Petrarchan tradition, while much of his inspiration may be traced to the Latin poetry of the humanists, particularly that of Marullus and Johannes Secundus. Derivative as he was, he at least displayed more originality than Olivier de Baguy, though this forgotten poet's contemporaries ranked his *Amours* (1553) with Ronsard and Du Bellay.

By this time Petrarchism was the dominating force in the French lyric and so it remained for several decades. Despite Du Bellay's eventual rebellion, voiced in his *A une Dame*, the tradition still went on, now turning to Bembo, now even to the Quattrocentisti. It was a cult of imitation, but an imitation which eventually became as spontaneous as a series of variations on a set theme. Attempts to break away from Petrarch's domination were neither whole-hearted nor lasting. As far as the lyric was concerned, the Renaissance in France was pure Petrarchism. In Germany it was another matter altogether; in fact, the absence there of Petrarchism before the seventeenth century suggests that there was no true literary Renaissance in Germany during the sixteenth century.

French Petrarchism had relied mostly on the Italian imitators of Petrarch. English Petrarchism depended considerably, though by no means entirely, on French Petrarchism. Something of Petrarch's own achievement had been known in England since the time of Chaucer, whose *Troilus and Chryseide* contains a rendering of one of Petrarch's sonnets. But it was Petrarch the humanist who was really known in fourteenth- and fifteenth-century England. For a thorough knowledge of Petrarch the poet it is necessary to wait until the reign of Henry VIII, when the impact of the Renaissance had made Italian fashions popular over here. Until then the structure of the English lyric had remained stiffly medieval, and even Skelton's verse, despite its humanist veneer, betrays a hand accustomed to a Gothic rather than an italianate style.

The influence of Petrarch and his followers proved a mixed blessing in England. It encouraged artificiality and insincerity and an exaggerated idea of the importance of form. On the other hand, it enriched diction and improved technique; it led to the rejection of antiquated rhetorical values and revolutionized metrics beyond recognition. Here, too, Petrarch's influence came both directly from his poems and indirectly through his Italian and French imitators. Wyatt, for instance, was influenced by Marot and Mellin de Saint-Gelais, while at a later stage Sidney was considerably indebted to Ronsard and Desportes. Spenser's Platonism essentially came from Italy, even though he also fell under the influence of Marot, Du Bellay, and Ronsard. Later English Petrarchism, however, from Sidney in the 1580s to Drummond of Hawthornden in the early seventeenth century, relied mostly on France.

Whatever faint echoes of Petrarch may be heard in English poetry between Chaucer and Skelton, it was really with Sir Thomas Wyatt (1503–1542) that English Petrarchism made its appearance. In some ways his approach to Petrarch was not so different from the humanist approach to Cicero. What he sought in him was, above all, a repertory of conceits, fine phrases, and rhetorical tricks. With his marked taste for the flamboyant, it is scarcely surprising that the lyrics of Petrarch which appealed most to him were those now considered the most artificial. Wyatt's taste for Petrarch was stimulated, if not actually initiated, by his visit to Italy in 1527; and the depth of his appeal is shown by the fact that no less than ten of his thirty-eight sonnets were virtual translations of sonnets by Petrarch. The Petrarchists of late-fifteenth-century Italy also left their mark on his poetry, as well as both Marot and Mellin de Saint-Gelais. Other Italians who influenced him were Luigi Alamanni and

Pietro Aretino. Wyatt's satire on the courtier's life is clearly modelled upon the tenth satire of Alamanni, while Aretino's prose rendering inspired his version of the seven penitential psalms in 'terza rima'.

In more ways than one, Wyatt is comparable to Boscán, the Spanish Renaissance lyricist. Both writers suffered from a deficiency of imagination and had difficulty in coping with language and metre. A comparison between Wyatt's and Surrey's renderings of Petrarch's sonnet 'Amor che nel pensier mio vive e regna' reveals their respective approaches to that poet. Wyatt's lyrics never rose above mere artificiality. Yet, with all his weaknesses, it was Wyatt who sowed the seeds of the courtly Renaissance lyric in England. Almost certainly, he introduced the eight-line stanza, the 'terza rima', and, most important of all, the sonnet. His sonnets, however, are closer in structure to those of Marot than to Italian models, and often consist of three four-line stanzas with a final epigrammatic couplet.

The same sonnet-structure was also employed by Surrey (Henry Howard, Earl of Surrey 1518–1547), whose English version of the second book of the *Aeneid*, very probably modelled on Francesco Maria Molza's poetic translation of two books of that poem, introduced blank verse into English poetry. Surrey's sonnets consist of three four-line stanzas with varied rhyme schemes, and a couplet at the end. He never visited Italy; yet he showed an excellence of taste, particularly evident in his diction, which is free from archaisms and borrowings from Latin. To Surrey the love lyric was, above all, a formal exercise. Some of his sonnets were translations from Petrarch's *Canzoniere*, others he based on Ariosto. His diction shows many debts to Petrarch's. So successfully did he assimilate Italian poetry that his versions from Petrarch and other Italians were not much inferior in quality to their originals.

Historically Wyatt and Surrey were to English literature what Boscán and Garcilaso de la Vega were to Spanish. It was not until Watson's *Ecalompathia* and Sidney's *Astrophel and Stella* that a fresh chapter opened in English Petrarchism, and with these two poets we are well into the reign of Elizabeth I. In the interim Petrarch's influence may be seen, it is true, in the *Miscellany* issued in 1557 by Richard Tottel, but the book marks no step forward, in spite of the preface's claim that England could now show poets as refined as the Latins and the Italians. The verse of Wyatt and Surrey figures prominently in the volume. Other contributors include Nicholas Grimald, whose forty lyrics reveal only a polished classical diction; Thomas Heywood; and Lord Vaux, a courtier of the time of Henry VIII who had been closely associated with Wyatt and Surrey. English Petrarchism came of age when the Italian Renaissance was really over and the Baroque well on its way. Yet its first spokesmen in the England of Henry VIII quickly overcame their initial difficulties: the use of metres which were unfamiliar, and not designed for the English language in any case; and alien conceptions of poetry and rhetoric.

These were difficulties which proved common to other literatures outside Italy. Spain, however, had an advantage in its long tradition of Petrarchan imitation. Spanish acceptance of Petrarchism was only one aspect of the general cultural orientation towards Italy so evident in the country during the fifteenth and sixteenth centuries. When mentioning Spain we must, however, remember that it was not unified until 1479, when Castile and Aragon became a single monarchy under Ferdinand and Isabella. Before then the Iberian Peninsula was divided not only politically but also culturally. Auziàs March (*c.* 1397–1459), the Valencian poet, never considered himself a Spaniard, nor did he write in Castilian but in his own native Valencian Catalan. Whether he was subjected to Petrarch's influence, and to what degree, is still a controversial matter, since the Petrarchan element in his verse might equally well be derived from the troubadoric lyric of Provence, to which Petrarch himself was considerably indebted. The poetry of March is still medieval enough to be obsessed by the idea of death, and to speak in praise of poverty. His romantic quest for a great and pure love fulfilled itself in two marriages and a succession of mistresses, but there was a puritan streak in him which kept him from even mentioning the beauty of his lady in his poetry.

Love in his lyric poetry is Platonic and, in accordance with courtly tradition, addressed to a lady who is already married, one Doña Teresa. Beyond the exaltation of this passion, the real aim of his tormented poetry was to work out the contradictions of love and explain its mysteries. His verse, often obscure, is characterized by a gloom and pessimism which is relieved only by his sincere religious feeling. He found no place for Petrarchan ornament; for his poetic sources he turned to the Troubadours and particularly to Arnaut Daniel and his 'trobar clus'. For his philosophical background he relied on the theologians of the later Middle Ages and on Dante. For echoes of Petrarch we must look to Jordi de Sant Jordi—the last in the line of Valencian poetry, since Valencia seems to have lost its own literary language after the union with Castile.

In fifteenth-century Castile Dante remained the main foreign influence on Juan de Mena. The first entrance of Petrarchan influence is to be found in Inigo López de Mendoza, Marquis of Santillana (1398–1458), whose mastery of traditional native forms did not prevent him from studying the poets of France and Italy. It is true that the poetry of Santillana, with its didactic and rhetorical emphasis, is still rigidly medieval, particularly in the longer poems. Here, and in his courtly poems, he does not show himself to best advantage. It is his *Serranillas* which have ensured him a lasting place in Spanish letters. The Petrarchan element in his work shows itself in his early use of hendecasyllabics on the Italian model, and in his adoption of the sonnet form.

Santillana was, however, an isolated instance and founded no tradition. Even his nephew, Jorge Manrique, owed nothing to Petrarch in his verse. Later Torres Naharro, an

Estremaduran who lived in Rome and wrote some sonnets in Italian, felt the influence of Petrarch and the late-fifteenth-century writers of 'strambotti', as is shown in the lyrics of his *Propalliada* (1517), but again the example went unfollowed.

Petrarchism really made its appearance in Spain with Juan Boscán (c. 1495–1542), a Catalan brought up in Castile at the court of Ferdinand and Isabella. He was a born poetic innovator, and his 'carta' to the Duchess of Soma indicates that he was fully conscious of his role. It seems unlikely that he knew the Petrarchan poems of Santillana, for they were not available in print during his lifetime. It is, on the other hand, certain that it was his meeting in Granada in 1528 with Andrea Navagero, the Venetian envoy to Charles V, that proved the decisive moment in his literary career and in the history of Spanish poetry. For Navagero, besides being an accomplished diplomat, was also (after Bembo) the leading Venetian humanist of his time. His own poetic production consisted mostly of exquisite Latin verse, but as an intimate of Bembo he was no stranger to vernacular poetry. It was in fact on this subject that he first spoke with Boscán. Judging correctly where the Spaniard's interests lay, he induced him to try his hand at writing sonnets as well as verse in the other metric forms of Italy. The lyrics which Boscán produced included both sonnets and 'canzoni'; moreover, he also experimented with the 'terza rima', though he found great difficulty in adopting this form to the Spanish language.

Despite Boscán's significance in literary history, he was a poor poet. His versification remained flat and pedestrian, in complete contrast to the magnificent prose of his Castilian rendering of Castiglione's *Cortegiano*. In poetry all he derived from the Italians was the external forms. His imitation of Petrarch's 'canzone', *chiare fresche e dolci acque*, is only a pale shadow of the original, while when he tried his hand at paraphrasing the thirty-five stanzas which Bembo had written in Urbino for the Carnival of 1507 his version ran to a full hundred stanzas more than his model. The difference between him and Garcilaso de la Vega (1501–1537) is immense, for Garcilaso was a genuinely great poet.

Just at the time when Boscán was meeting Navagero in Granada, Garcilaso was at work in Italy, experimenting for himself with the new metrical forms. Actually he had the benefit of Boscán's advice in selecting the metres in which he recorded his unhappy love for Doña Isabel Freire. The later years of his short life were also spent in Italy, and there he steeped himself in the Renaissance. Italian influence on him was thus not limited to Petrarch and the 'petrarchists'. The first of his eclogues is very close to the twelfth eclogue of Sannazzaro, whose famous sonnet on Icarus he also turned into Spanish. His allegiance to Petrarch, in fact, did not last very long. As he developed as a poet, he turned to Politian and Bernardo Tasso, as well as to Sannazzaro, for fresh inspiration. In every case he went far beyond mere imitation of these writers, and his elegies, songs, and sonnets represent a real transformation of his models into a highly original poetry of his own. The least rhetorical of stylists, he wrote a highly musical verse, endowed with an elegance and purity of diction hitherto unknown in Spain. His language blended the straightforwardness of prose with the sensitivity of poetry, avoiding affectation without degenerating into dryness. Garcilaso created modern Spanish poetry, and every sixteenth-century Spanish poet after him was his pupil. The fusion of the Italian and Spanish poetic traditions was taken further by the Governor of Siena, Don Diego Hurtado de Mendoza, who wrote verse both in the Spanish and in the Italian way. But it was only during the reign of Philip II (1555–98), in the 'siglo de oro', that Spanish Petrarchism entered a new phase.

Parallel to the development of Petrarchism in Spain was its rise in Portugal. Faint echoes of Petrarch may be detected in some early-sixteenth-century Portuguese poetry. With Francisco Sà de Miranda's sojourn in Italy (1521–6), the Portuguese lyric ceased to be medieval and became Petrarchan. The time was ripe for the introduction of Italian influence, and the adoption of Italian metres was the first step. Sà de Miranda proclaimed Petrarch as his model, but Petrarch was not the only Italian poet he followed. Dante, Sannazzaro, Bembo, Ariosto, Rucellai, and Lattanzio Tolomei also left their mark on his work. His lyrics acquired their subjects, attitudes, and rhetoric from Italy, yet he succeeded in retaining his own poetic personality. In view of his difficulties as an innovator, it is not surprising that his diction never attained any real elegance or refinement, and that his metre remained halting (his hendecasyllables, in particular, are laboured). His outlook was that of a humanist, but only up to a point. For his moralizing, his contempt of worldly vanities, and his tendency to asceticism all had a medieval flavour and counteracted the Platonic element in his thinking. He was, however, the teacher of the Portuguese Petrarchists. Antonio Ferreira (1528–1569), who wrote his collection of love lyrics in Italian metres, surpassed his master in formal elegance and revealed an obvious sincerity or feeling, while the *Flores de Lima* of Diogo Bernardez contained an impressive sequence of faultless Petrarchan sonnets. Nor were they the only Portuguese devotees of Petrarch. Besides these two, there were many other Petrarchists up to the time of Camoens, though their significance is historical rather than poetic.

Portuguese Petrarchism reached its climax with Luís de Camoens (1524–1580). In him the old poetic forms of Gil Vicente and the new ones of Sà de Miranda were blended with all that was best in Garcilaso and the Petrarchists of sixteenth-century Italy. A great artist as well as a true poet, Camoens employed the flamboyant imagery and diction of the Petrarchists and yet remained entirely original. In this respect he resembles Garcilaso or Tasso.

The lyric poetry of Camoens deals mostly, though not entirely, with love and its tribulations. True, he achieves a profound pathos in those sonnets in which he mourns the deaths of his friends, but he is at his greatest when giving expression to the anxiety and despair of unhappy love. The themes of his *Rimas* are conventional: separation, inconstancy, the cruelty of the beloved, and so forth. These are presented by him sometimes tenderly, sometimes vigorously, but invariably with a richness and variety of diction which never loses spontaneity and freshness, and which is just as much at its ease when sounding the depths of passion as when dealing with the refinements of courtly love. Some of his sonnets, like the one 'Clara minha inimiga' for his drowned Chinese mistress, or the one for the death of Catharina de Athaide, rank among the most moving poems in European literature.

All the world of Camoens may be found in his poetry. The countryside in the glory of spring, and the Tagus thronged with nymphs, the courtly splendour of Lisbon, and the wars against the Moors, all figure in his lyrics; while thoughts of the Far East and the ocean inspired him to write his great epic *Os Lusiadas*.

# 9
# Pastoral literature and drama outside Italy

THE yearning for a golden age was a persistent feature of classical literature. Despite the coming of Christianity, the same dream haunted the Renaissance. Arcadia was thought of as a classical Garden of Eden, a lost paradise peopled by shepherds who really had very little of the pastoral about them. The classical Latin eclogue had never been forgotten in Western Europe, and Virgil's *Bucolics* were sedulously read during the Middle Ages, and in particular the fourth of them, which was believed to foretell the coming of Christ. Dante, Petrarch, and Boccaccio thus wrote their Latin eclogues in a living tradition. Nevertheless, it was Petrarch's work in this form that made the writing of Latin eclogues popular, and influenced a swarm of humanists to try their hand, both in his lifetime and during the fifteenth and sixteenth centuries. Eclogues in the vernacular also made their first appearance in Italy during the fifteenth century. Moreover, some pastoral genres were already popular in vernacular literature during the later Middle Ages, when the 'pastourelle' was a much cultivated poetic form in France, practised also in Provence and Italy, and when the mystery plays and farces had their shepherd interludes.

Among Boccaccio's Italian writings the nymphs and shepherds of his *Ninfale d'Ameto* and *Ninfale Fiesolano* started a new literary fashion. This was cultivated in the *Arcadia* of Sannazzaro, the romance which proved so strong an influence on England, France, and Spain. Some years even before the *Arcadia*, Politian had written his *Orfeo*, a play which in some ways anticipated the pastoral drama, a form which found its first true expression in the *Sacrificio* of Agostino Beccari (1553), though to see it at its best we have to wait until the following generation with the appearance of Tasso's *Aminta* and Guarini's *Pastor Fido*.

The pastoral tradition in French medieval literature had already shown its vitality during the second half of the thirteenth century with *Li Jeus de Robin et Marion* by Adam de la Halle—performed, incidentally, for the first time in Naples, which since 1266 had been under a French monarchy. During the fifteenth century both 'pastourelles' and mystery plays remained popular in France, and when humanism began to exert its influence there Virgilian eclogues appeared alongside the *Calendrier des Bergers*. Fausto Andrelini (the Italian humanist who settled in France in the 1480s under the patronage of Charles VIII, and later became the court poet of Louis XII) was the author of several Latin eclogues on contemporary themes which enjoyed wide popularity. Among their imitators was Johannes Arnolletus. The most popular Latin eclogues, however, in early Renaissance France were those of the Italian humanist, Battista Mantovano. His poems were even more popular than those of Virgil himself, and were regularly reprinted in France from 1488 onwards. This does not mean, of course, that the eclogues of Virgil were overlooked. In fact, the earliest surviving work by Clément Marot is a French verse translation of Virgil's first eclogue, the *Tityre*, made in 1513 or 1514. Not long after, the whole of Virgil's *Bucolics* was turned into French by Guillaume Michel de Tours. Admittedly, this version is of indifferent quality, yet its appearance reflects the prevalent interest in pastoral poetry, characteristic of the humanist rather than the medieval tradition. The medieval was, however, far from extinct. In 1517, when Guillaume Crétin wrote the first original eclogue in French in celebration of the birth of the

Dauphin, he chose to blend classical and medieval elements. On the other hand, if we turn to the magnificent eclogue by Marot, written in September 1531 to mourn the death of Louise of Savoy, the mother of King Francis I, we find hardly any medieval features. The influence here is clearly Virgilian; the whole eclogue is an ingenious series of variations on Virgilian themes, with a poetic freshness that looks forward to Ronsard. Other eclogues that came out of the italianate court of Francis I were by Luigi Alamanni, a Florentine refugee who enjoyed a great vogue at the court and published his Italian eclogues at Lyons.

French eclogues were also composed outside the sphere of the court. The *Arion* (1532) and the *Saulsaye* (1547) by Maurice Scève and the *Eclogue Marine* (1547) by Hugues Salel indicate that even in the provinces there were writers aware of the new literary fashions. But between Marot and Ronsard there is little of lasting importance. In view of Ronsard's exceptional poetic powers in other directions, his eclogues are, it is true, somewhat disappointing. Their poetry is essentially courtly; the shepherds and shepherdesses are transparent disguises for princes and princesses, or sometimes for the author and his friends. In fact, although these eclogues are superior to anything before, they must strike the reader as monotonous and artificial.

As in Italy, so in France the eclogue led eventually to the development of pastoral drama. We must, however, wait until 1566 for the first pastoral drama in French to appear. This was *Les Ombres* by Nicolas Filleul, which was performed at the Castle of Gaillon before Charles IX and his mother, Queen Catherine de Medici.

In Spain the eclogue also won the attention of the greatest Renaissance poets. A non-classical pastoral tradition had been flourishing in the country during the later Middle Ages and had found its expression in lyric poetry (e.g. in that of the Marquis of Santillana) and in certain of the mystery plays. What is more, the *Bucolics* of Virgil were well known and in 1490 Juan de Encina completed his vernacular translation of these poems. The same author wrote eclogues of his own in a sufficiently dramatic form to be acted; but neither these nor the eclogues of Lucas Fernández are important except historically.

It was Garcilaso de la Vega who produced the finest eclogues in the whole of Renaissance literature. He did not attempt to make his characters talk like real shepherds, but this is immaterial. What is remarkable is their obviously sincere feeling. In a genre so prone to artificiality Garcilaso never failed to be natural and spontaneous. His rhythm expresses his mood perfectly; his language is musical. All this may be seen at its best in his third eclogue, which was also his last poem and was written in Naples, since with it the poet, whose real masters had been Politian and Sannazzaro rather than Petrarch, achieved a perfection greater than any of them.

In France the eclogue had paved the way for pastoral drama. In Spain it led to the pastoral novel, the first of which, Jorge de Montemayor's *Diana*, was also the best. In 1547 a Spanish version of Sannazzaro's *Arcadia* had been issued in Toledo, and the *Diana* is clearly based on Sannazzaro's romance. This is evident not only from its structure but also from the flowery character of its prose. Like the *Arcadia*, Montemayor's *Diana* suffers from an involved plot and excessive digressions. Nevertheless, from its first appearance in 1559, or thereabouts, it proved an enormous success and served as a model for a long succession of pastoral novels, from the *Diana* of Alfonso Pérez (1564) onwards.

The unusual popularity of pastoral poetry in Spain did not extend to Portugal. At the very end of the fifteenth century a few Latin eclogues were written by Henrique Cayado; but he was in Bologna at the time, studying under such distinguished humanist masters as the elder Beroaldo and Codro Urceo, and the poems had no influence whatever upon literature at home. The situation was similar in Germany. Here the Latin eclogues of Eobanus Hess and those by Euricius Cordus are typical humanist productions, behind which the shadow of Battista Mantovano is clearly perceptible; but they exerted no influence on vernacular letters.

On the other hand, in England we find that the Renaissance pastoral tradition, which became an important element with Spenser and Sidney, was already alive in 1514. Alexander Barclay, who had previously made an English version of Sebastian Brant's *Narrenschiff* (not from the German original but from the Latin version of it by Jacob Locher), in that year published his English eclogues. With these, pastoral poetry was launched in England. Barclay differed, however, from pastoral writers in other countries, whose eclogues were generally either erotic, allegorical, encomiastic, or religious in tone. With Barclay the tone was instead moralizing and satirical, and reminiscent of some of the Latin eclogues of the humanists, such as Andrelini's *De fuga Balbi*.

In his eclogues Barclay replaced the conventional names handed down from the classical pastoral with English names. The country life, too, is English and not 'Arcadian'. But his sources were quite clearly humanistic. The eclogues of Battista Mantovano were his principal model. He is indebted to them for his characterization, as well as for the subject-matter of his fourth and fifth eclogues. The miseries of court life were the subject of the first three, and for this theme he drew on the *De Miseria Curialium* by Aeneas Sylvius. None the less, the persons and events he describes are drawn unmistakably from Henry VIII's England and not Frederick III's Germany.

The popularity of pastoral poetry in Europe was partly due to the taste for allegory which had survived the Middle Ages, but it was also due to the way it enabled everyday reality to be presented in an idealized setting. The poet could conjure up a golden age which, although mythical, nevertheless represented the aspirations of people to whom classical antiquity was the secular side of revealed truth. The fact that eclogues could be acted, as indeed they often were, added to their popularity, and served to stimulate the rise of the drama proper.

Although the first Senecan tragedy, the *Ecerinis* by Mussato, was written as early as 1315, and imitations of Plautus and Terence were often written in Italy during the fifteenth century, it was not until 1508 that Ariosto produced his *Cassaria*, the first classical comedy in Italian. Trissino's *Sofonisba*, the first classical tragedy in Italian, was written as late as 1515. On the other hand, during the first half of the sixteenth century the French dramatic field was still dominated by the lay 'moralities', which mostly took the form of allegories or parables. Some even portrayed historical events. Besides these there were also the miracle plays and the farces. With the spread of the Reformation to France, a curious situation arose. Orthodox Catholics now saw in all these plays instruments for spreading heresy and satirizing the Church, whereas the reformers proved just as hostile for entirely different reasons. Eventually, in 1548, the Parliament of Paris went so far as to forbid the Fraternity of the Passion to perform their mystery plays for fear of the propagation of unorthodox views.

Plays in French on the classical pattern were late in appearing, even though in 1514 the humanist Quintianus Stoa had published two of his Latin tragedies in Paris. In early-sixteenth-century France, Latin plays were read rather than performed, apart from a few performances staged privately by the pupils of schools or colleges. With the spread of Greek, tragedies in that language also began to be known. Erasmus's Latin version of two tragedies by Euripides was printed in Paris in 1507. Nevertheless, it was only in 1529 or thereabouts that Lazaire de Baïf issued his French translation of Sophocles's *Electra*. In 1536 came the publication of Alamanni's Italian version of the *Antigone*, while in 1554 Trissino's *Sofonisba* was adapted by Saint-Gelais for performance at court. The Latin tragedies of the Scotsman George Buchanan also left a mark on the French theatre, but the first native classical tragedy in French did not appear before the winter of 1552–3, when the *Cléopatre* of Etiénne Jodelle was first performed.

The *Cléopatre*, modelled on the tragedies of Seneca, was both rhetorical and sententious. Its historical source was Plutarch's life of Antony and it was badly written and virtually devoid of action, yet it had its importance since it marked a complete breakaway from medieval tradition. It was in five acts, separated by choral songs, and the chorus also participated in the dialogue. An imitation of Seneca's *Agamemnon* by Charles Tourtain, published in 1556, showed that the real influence on French tragedy was Senecan rather than Greek. Only the *César* of Jacques Grévin (1560), though modelled upon Muretus's *Julius Caesar* (1544), made a real effort to improve upon the model by introducing new elements, drawn from Plutarch's lives of Antony and Brutus.

More or less contemporary with the rise of classical tragedy in France was the rise of classical comedy. Hitherto, the comic stage had been monopolized by medieval farces and Italian comedies, and these were to prove the main influence upon the French comic theatre. For the moment Italian humanist comedies proved very popular. Ariosto's *Suppositi* was turned into French verse in 1545 by Jacques Bourgeois and into French prose seven years later by Jean Pierre de Mesne; later a French translation of another of Ariosto's Italian comedies, the *Negromante*, was made by Jean de la Taille. A few years earlier, in 1543, *Gli ingannati*, one of the comedies produced by the Academy of the Intronati of Siena, had appeared in French, and enjoyed enough success to be published again in 1549 and 1556. Again, the brilliant but obscene *Calandria* by Cardinal Bibbiena, which had delighted the court of Pope Leo X, was performed by Italian actors in Lyons before Queen Catherine de Medici in 1548.

The need for a vernacular comedy, modelled upon the ancients but modern in tone, was particularly strongly felt

THE SPREAD OF ITALIAN HUMANISM

by Etiénne Jodelle. Yet his comedy the *Eugène*, first performed before the court in 1552, proved to be a direct descendant of the medieval farce, in spite of the claims he made in the prologue. Its plot has none of the intricacies of classical and humanist comedy. The example of Jodelle was followed by Jacques Grévin, the author of *César*. His *La Trésorière* (1558) would not have been possible without *Eugène*, just as his *Les Esbahis* is clearly derived from Charles Estienne's translation of *Gli ingannati*. Thus in the field of comedy Renaissance France had no more to show than a few experiments. Here Spain certainly proved far more original than France.

The modern Spanish theatre begins with a masterpiece, *La Celestina* or *Tragicomedia de Calisto y Melibea* by Fernando de Rojas (*c.* 1474–1541), first published in Burgos in 1499. The *Celestina* caught the attention of Europe immediately. Whether it is a play in the true sense is a matter of opinion. Although it is in dialogue form and divided into acts, sixteen in the first edition, twenty-two in that of 1502, in many ways it resembles a dramatized novel rather than a play. Its author was undoubtedly a man of wide culture, who brought his experience of classical and humanist literature to bear on the spirit of the work, if not on its form; though here, too, both Petrarch and Terence have contributed something. What makes this tragic story of two lovers unique is its successful combination of intensity and restraint. Celestina, the procuress, a formidable personality, is a deep and subtle representation of a hypocrisy which remains always human and never degenerates into a mere personification of vice. The variety, the tragic power, the vivacity of the dialogue, the intense realism with which the author presents the miseries of everyday life, deserve prolonged study. Admittedly, artificiality is not altogether absent. Yet the author's deep humanity makes *La Celestina* the greatest drama in the two thousand years between the Greek tragedians and Shakespeare.

The *Celestina* naturally had many imitators, but none

came near to it in quality. The *Penitencia de Amor* of Manuel Jimenez de Urria lacked its humanity and tragic power, while Juan de Encina's dramas and those of his followers, Lucas Fernández and Torres Naharro, were merely dull and insipid. In fact, after *La Celestina* no plays of any real merit were written in Spanish until we come to Lope de Vega.

The *Celestina* also had some influence in Portugal. The comedies by Jorge Ferreira de Vasconcellos (d. 1585), the *Euphrosina, Ulyssippo*, and *Aulegraphia*, are feeble imitations, written in a prose which is both complex and obscure. It is a different matter with Gil Vicente (*c.* 1465–1536?), who wrote both in Portuguese and Spanish. Although he began by copying the eclogues of Encina and was also deeply influenced by Erasmus, he openly followed medieval tradition in his *Autos*, and derived the subject-matter of his two tragicomedies, the *Amadis de Gaula* and the *Dom Duartes*, from the romances of chivalry. Everything he wrote, even his farces, revealed the hand of a great writer, the greatest produced by Portugal before Camoens.

In the German-speaking world religious drama practically monopolized the medieval stage, but by the early sixteenth century it was slowly declining. Its only competitors had been the so-called 'Shrovetide plays', coarse farces of a satirical type written in doggerel verse without any division into acts. Hans Sachs (1494–1576) wrote eighty-five of these and introduced many refinements. During the first half of the sixteenth century, however, there was a movement towards classical drama inspired by the rise of humanism. The actual beginnings of German classical drama can be traced to the German students who attended Italian universities and were anxious to put on performances at home of the classical plays they had seen in Italy. Many of these scholars sympathized with Luther and his doctrines, so that the developing vernacular drama became a vehicle for the teachings of the Reformers. Meanwhile, however, there were the Latin plays of the humanists. These were invariably in five acts, and were written by well-known figures like Jacob Locher and Conrad Celtis (the discoverer of Hroswitha's plays). But of all these Latin plays the only one worth remembering now is the *Henno* or *Scaenica progymnasmata* (1497) of Johann Reuchlin, which was first performed by the students at Heidelberg. The form and structure of the *Henno* came straight from Terence; it also included choruses, which never occur in Roman comedy and were derived from the tragedies of Seneca. Yet, for all this, it was, as far as subject-matter went, a typical peasants' farce of the later Middle Ages, a Shrovetide play in classical attire.

When we turn to German vernacular drama we find that it was of two kinds, each restricted to a particular audience. On the one hand there were the popular plays meant for performance in market squares; on the other there was the classical drama written by schoolmasters who had read and taught Terence. The first German play influenced by the classical tradition was *Der verlorne Sohn* by Burkard Valdis, which, appearing as it did in 1527, was also the earliest Protestant drama based on a biblical subject. It still retained features of the Shrovetide plays, but its division into five acts and the use of choruses betray the impact of the New Learning. A more definite effort to conform to classical tradition was evident seven years later in the *Susanna* of Paul Rebhun. This play followed ancient dramatic structure very closely, particularly in the choruses. In neighbouring Switzerland two biblical dramas on strict classical lines appeared in 1532: the *Funferlei Betrachtnisse* of Johann Kolross and the *Susanna* of Sixt Berck.

In England the origins of the new drama were definitely courtly. The English medieval stage had been monopolized by mystery plays and moralities, but during the reign of Henry VIII the first dramas on classical or humanist lines began to appear. It is somewhat surprising that this did not happen earlier. The earliest commentary on Seneca's tragedies, or at any rate the earliest which has come down to us, was the work of an English Dominican who flourished during the first half of the fourteenth century, Nicholas Trevet. Seneca's tragedies were well known to fifteenth-century English humanists. The same may be said for the comedies of Terence, which were also read in schools, and a master at Magdalen College School, Oxford, John Anwykyll, even published in 1483 a selection of 'sentences' extracted from his plays and translated into English. Later, 'interludes' were performed in the houses of great prelates; Henry Medwall, one of the chaplains of Cardinal Morton, Archbishop of Canterbury, wrote one called *Nature* (printed in 1538 and also translated into Latin) and another called *Fulgens and Lucrece*. The latter's plot was taken from the *Declamatio de vera nobilitate* by Bonaccorso da Montemagno, but it added a comic underplot, in which the suitors' servants were rivals for the favours of the heroine's maid.

There were also performances of classical comedies: a comedy by Plautus was given in 1520 for the entertainment of some French hostages; the same author's *Phormio* and *Menaechmi* was acted at St. Paul's School in 1527 and 1528 respectively. An English translation of Terence's *Andria* appeared, moreover, in 1530. None the less, it was only during the second half of the sixteenth century that classical influence became really effective. The plays of John Heywood, who was a member of the Household of Henry VIII, were English counterparts of the French farces and were mainly characterized by lack of action and development. As for *A new commedye in Englysh in manner of an interlude*, issued in 1530, this was no more than a verse adaptation of the earlier sections of the *Celestina*. Again, the so-called 'comedies' of John Bale, of which only five out of twenty-two have survived, were really Protestant propaganda. They can be classed as mystery plays—and dull ones at that, though mercifully short. Even Bale's *King Johan*, where King John is made the hero because of his fight with the Papacy, is monotonous and lifeless, despite the possibilities of its theme. In fact, it was not until we reach

Nicholas Udall, Headmaster of Eton from 1534 to 1541, that characters straight out of Plautine comedy first appeared on the English stage. Similarly, the first tragedy in English did not make its appearance until about 1562. This, the highly declamatory *Gordobuc* by Thomas Norton and Thomas Sackville, duly introduced the chorus but utterly disregarded unity of time. The play is typical of the intense interest in classical and Renaissance drama taken by the early Elizabethans, an interest which is emphasized by the various English translations of tragedies by Seneca, as well as by George Gascoigne's versions of Ariosto's *Suppositi* and Dolce's *Giocasta*. These were indeed paving the way for the wonderful outburst of drama in the next generation.

# Renaissance fiction

FICTION as an art was very much alive during the later Middle Ages. It generally took the form either of lengthy narrative poems about Charlemagne and his peers, or of prose romances dealing with the deeds of King Arthur and his Knights, or with the so-called matter of Troy or Rome. There were also narrative poems of an allegorical kind, such as the *Roman de la Rose* and *Piers Plowman*, and shorter stories in prose and verse, such as the French 'fabliaux'. With the exception of the 'fabliaux', each of these forms was adopted and modified by the Renaissance. Thus the long narrative poems gave birth to the chivalric romances, while the prose narratives developed into novels, in some cases very little different in structure from novels today. The shorter stories tended to become longer and more involved, instead of being merely elaborate anecdotes as in the past.

In Italy the short story was born with Boccaccio. He also wrote romances, but it was really Sannazzaro's *Arcadia*, Colonna's *Hypnerotomachia Poliphili*, and Caviceo's *Libro del Peregrino* that launched the Renaissance novel, just as it was Boiardo's *Orlando Innamorato* rather than Pulci's *Morgante Maggiore* that provided the first example of a Renaissance chivalric romance. With Italy, then, we are on firm ground. But when did Renaissance fiction actually start outside Italy? As far as England is concerned, it is argued that there was no Renaissance fiction before Lyly's

*Euphues*, Sidney's *Arcadia*, or Spenser's *Faery Queene*. With these works, however, we are well into the reign of Elizabeth I, which is not normally considered part of the Renaissance. On the other hand 'Renaissance' has become so elastic a period that it tends to become stretched in time in either direction. What, then, of Chaucer's *Canterbury Tales* and Malory's *Morte Darthur*? No one can deny Chaucer's debt to Petrarch and Boccaccio. But he never went beyond the borrowing of subject-matter together with an occasional image or rhetorical device. In spirit he remained completely medieval to the end, just as Dante three generations before him. Malory, too, for all his skill as a narrator and his lively imagination, never strayed from the traditions of the medieval Arthurian romance.

Notwithstanding the rise of humanism, a medieval atmosphere still prevailed in sixteenth-century German literature. Hans Sachs, who died as late as 1576, is still thoroughly medieval in taste and technique, and the only Renaissance feature of the autobiographical romances written under the name of the Emperor Maximilian I (1493–1519), the *Theuerdank* and the *Weisskunig*, are the superb illustrations of their first editions. In fact, outside Italy only two countries really provided 'modern' fiction during the Renaissance: France and Spain.

In France public taste remained fascinated by medieval fiction. Even the *Girone il Cortese* of Luigi Alamanni is a Renaissance adaptation of a medieval French romance. We may note also the frequent reprinting of the old romances as well as the great success of such a thoroughly Gothic piece as the Spanish *Amadis of Gaul*. Prose, not poetry, was the field in which French Renaissance fiction operated. France did not produce an *Orlando Furioso*, but Rabelais's novel instead; and Rabelais (1494–1553) was the most typical, as well as the greatest, literary figure in the French Renaissanee. In him the new learning from Italy, the Latin classics, and the new knowledge of Greek, were absorbed into the medieval scholastic culture which was still the heart of French intellectual life. The man who with his coarse jesting laughed scholasticism out of the universities, nevertheless inherited a scholasticism of outlook, which he never abandoned. His great novel is like a Gothic cathedral which has been transformed into a Renaissance church without altogether losing its original structure. His humour is still that of the 'fabliaux' and the old farces; his ostentatious display of learning is typically scholastic. Yet his classical erudition, his common sense and moderation, his sympathy for the miseries of man, certainly do not belong to the Middle Ages. Like Erasmus, he was a monk for some time in his life; and the two Italian writers who exerted the strongest influence upon him, Teofilo Folengo and Francesco Colonna, were also members of the regular clergy—though, like Rabelais himself, no paragons of monastic virtue.

Behind the romance of Rabelais stand the burlesque epics written in macaronic Latin by Folengo. Rabelais's *Panurge* is in fact a French version of Folengo's *Cingar*, but flavoured with a humour that is entirely French. Quite frequently the gaiety of Rabelais degenerates into buffoonery, and he achieves absurdity rather than wit. On the other hand, as a satirist he is peerless. His satire owes its uniqueness to one quality: it never becomes personal (unlike Ariosto's, for example). The targets of Rabelais are not this prelate or that potentate, not even a particular class, but the whole of society. An exceptional insight into human nature enabled him to perceive and lay bare its weaknesses. In this he displayed a moderation and common sense not unlike Boccaccio's but illuminated by an imagination which was entirely his own. His use of language, despite a host of Greek and Latin borrowings, never loses its superb vitality and sparkle. Coarse and indecent he often was, and only too obviously revelled in being so. But we must not forget that the Renaissance attitude accepted as supremely comic what may strike us as grossly indecent. It was an age when the passages in *Lady Chatterley's Lover* which strike some readers today as unnecessarily crude would have either passed unnoticed or been taken as a form of light relief. Rabelais's romances at once proved popular. The frolics of his giants in a world which was not too dissimilar from the real world had a universal appeal. The humanists appreciated the immense classical learning behind these seemingly popular works, and particularly the way the author drew upon writers like Plutarch and Lucian. The less learned discovered in them something far more interesting and exciting than the old romances, in which the knights had endured their adventures without a spark of humour. But what, more than anything else, marked the adventures of Gargantua and Pantagruel was their exuberant and irrepressible vitality.

Compared with such a unique masterpiece, the *Héptameron* of Marguerite de Navarre (1492–1549) does not rank high. Yet had the romances of Rabelais never been written her collection of short stories would have had no real rival in French sixteenth-century fiction. When Marguerite began it there was already a strong tradition of short-story writing in France. Since Laurent de Premierfait had turned it into French during the late fourteenth century, Boccaccio's *Decameron* had enjoyed wide popularity. Again, in 1462, there appeared the *Cent nouvelle nouvelles*, an anonymous collection of short stories in French, which derived directly from Boccaccio's masterpiece and owed their success mainly to their reproduction of the more dubious elements in their original. Both the *Cent nouvelle nouvelles* and the *Decameron* were behind *Le Grand Parangon de nouvelle nouvelles* by Nicolas de Troyes (1537), an unfortunately mediocre work. Marguerite de Navarre's *Héptameron*, which was meant to be a new *Decameron*, was apparently conceived in 1541; but the work was only started in 1546, was still incomplete at her death, and was published only in 1558. It had been her intention to call the book 'Decameron'. The title *Héptameron* was given it by its second editor, Louis Gruget, only because it consisted of seventy-two stories. These stories were meant to be drawn from real life and not from other books. But this is certainly not the case with all of them. As in Sacchetti's *Novelle*, which she certainly never saw, each story is followed by an epilogue; but she was not in fact influenced by any Italian writer other than Boccaccio.

The *Héptameron* was the work of a natural story-teller. Yet for all its clear and unaffected style it remains of little interest to the modern reader. Despite Marguerite's ability to convey the essence of contemporary conversation, the tales do not succeed in capturing the vitality and atmosphere of Boccaccio's 'novelle', and when she tried her hand at pathos she is apt to degenerate into lifeless rhetoric. Though coarseness of language is not altogether absent, the moral tone is higher than in other Renaissance short stories. There are signs of Protestant bias, as well as a distinct prejudice against the mendicant orders. No doubt the exalted station of the author (she was sister to King Francis I and herself Queen of Navarre) contributed to the popularity of her work. But the fact that it had imitators shows that there were also more solid contemporary reasons for its popularity.

Spain had the distinction of inaugurating a new kind of fiction in the picaresque novel, the popularity of which was eventually to spread throughout the whole of Europe. Fiction had not been unknown in medieval Spain. The *Conde Lucanor* by Juan Manuel shows what Castile could produce in the age of Boccaccio. In fact, Boccaccio's romances themselves, as well as his ponderous Latin treatises, proved extremely popular in fifteenth-century Spain. His *Decameron* appeared in Spanish in 1496, followed by a version of the *Fiammetta* in 1497, yet Italian writers had little influence on the Spanish narrative tradition. As for the one Spanish chivalric romance which had a resounding success abroad, the *Amadis de Gaula* of Garcí Rodríguez de Montalvo, its success was due to its melodramatic character, rather than to its displaying the impact of the Renaissance upon the national romantic tradition.

So far as the novel was concerned there was no passage from the Middle Ages to the Renaissance in Spain. The transition was rather from medieval to modern; and the real successor of the *Amadis* and those other chivalric romances, which turned the head of poor Don Quixote, was the *Vida de Lazarillo de Tormes*, the publication of which in 1554 really inaugurated the picaresque novel. The *Vida* purports to be the autobiography of a boy from the slums of Salamanca. It consists of his adventures as a servant, first to a blind beggar, then to a miserly and impoverished priest, and finally to a squire whose only suit is the one he is wearing. The whole novel is permeated by an extreme realism which never shrinks from, and indeed seeks out, the more sordid sides of life. Yet humour there is in it, besides intense gusto and vitality and a keen sense of the dramatic. The *Vida* is an epic of low life, as imaginative as the best chivalric romances but on a realistic plane. Beggars are its unromantic heroes. There is continual fighting, but the fight is not for a great cause or against powerful enemies but for the next meal. In many ways this is the dawn of modern fiction.

A swift glance at the whole field of Renaissance fiction up to the middle of the Cinquecento reveals that Italy did not long remain in the forefront, except in the chivalric poem. In this genre Italy never lost its supremacy. Indeed, thanks to Tasso, this supremacy was still unchallenged even when the lights of the Renaissance were slowly fading. But in what we now call the novel, the main Italian contributions, Sannazzaro's *Arcadia* and the works by Colonna and Caviceo, are poor stuff compared with *La Celestina*, the *Vida de Lazarillo de Tormes*, or Rabelais's masterpiece. The common characteristic of these three works is their break with tradition. Theirs was a freedom which could have been brought about only by the Renaissance, and although European literature was not yet ready for Racine and Molière, Shakespeare and Cervantes were now only just round the corner. In fact, in an age when literary taste was personified by Lyly's *Euphues* in England, by Góngora's poetry in Spain, and Marino's in Italy, Shakespeare and Cervantes showed the world what wonders could be created from the legacy of the Renaissance.

# Bibliography

Rather than a real bibliography, the following is a concise list for further reading on the various aspects of the literary Renaissance discussed in this book. Whenever feasible, books in English have been given: periodical literature has been omitted entirely. An invaluable guide on recent publications may be found in the volumes of the *Year's Work in Modern Languages*.

*Chapter 1*

U. Cosmo, *A Handbook to Dante Studies* (Oxford, 1950)

P. Renucci, *L'Aventure de l'Humanisme Européen au Moyen Age* (Paris, 1953)

R. Weiss, *The Dawn of Humanism in Italy* (London, 1947)

*Chapter 2*

V. Branca, *Boccaccio Medievale* (Rome, 1956)

H. Hauvette, *Boccace* (Paris, 1914)

E. Hutton, *Giovanni Boccaccio—A Biographical Study* (London, 1909)

E. H. R. Tatham, *Francesco Petrarca: The First Man of Letters*, 2 vols. (London, 1925–6)

E. H. Wilkins, *Life of Petrarch* (Chicago, 1961)

*Chapter 3*

R. R. Bolgar, *The Classical Heritage and its Beneficiaries* (Cambridge, 1954)

J. Burckhardt, *The Civilization of the Renaissance in Italy* (New York, 1958)

E. Garin, *Die italienische Humanismus* (Bern, 1947)

E. Garin, *Medioevo e Rinascimento* (Bari, 1954)

D. Hay, *The Italian Renaissance in its Historical Background* (Cambridge, 1961)

R. Sabbadini, *Le scoperte dei codici latini e greci ne' secoli XIV e XV* (Florence, 1905)

R. Sabbadini, *Il metodo degli umanisti* (Florence, 1922)

B. Ullman, *The Humanism of Coluccio Salutati* (Padua, 1963)


*Chapter 4*

E. Cassirer, P. O. Kristeller, J. H. Randall, *The Renaissance Philosophy of Man* (Chicago, 1948)

R. Klibansky, *The Continuity of the Platonic Tradition during the Middle Ages* (London, 1939)

P. O. Kristeller, *The Philosophy of Marsilio Ficino* (New York, 1943)

P. O. Kristeller, *Renaissance Thought* (New York, 1961)

E. Renan, *Averroès et l'Averroisme* (Paris, 1867)

E. Troilo, *Averroismo e Aristotelismo Padovano* (Padua, 1939)


*Chapter 5*

E. Bertana, *La tragedia* (Milan, 1906)

F. Foffano, *Il poema cavalleresco* (Milan, 1905)

L. di Francia, *La novellistica* (Milan, 1924)

V. Rossi, *Il Quattrocento* (Milan, 1949)

I. Sanesi, *La commedia* (Milan, 1911)

N. Sapegno, *Il Trecento* (Milan, 1955)

J. H. Whitfield, *A Short History of Italian Literature* (Penguin Books, 1960)


*Chapter 6*

E. Carrara, *La poesia pastorale* (Milan, 1908)

J. Cartwright, *Baldassarre Castiglione* (London, 1908)

M. Catalano, *Vita di Ludovico Ariosto* (Geneva, 1931)

F. Chabod, *Machiavelli and the Renaissance* (Cambridge, Mass., 1958)

V. Cian, *Un illustre nunzio pontificio del Rinascimento: Baldassarre Castiglione* (Vatican City, 1951)

E. G. Gardner, *The King of Court Poets* (London, 1906)

D. E. Muir, *Machiavelli and his Times* (London, 1936)

E. Pércopo, *Vita di Jacopo Sannazzaro* (Naples, 1931)

## Chapter 7

M. Bataillon, *Érasme et l'Espagne* (Paris, 1937)

M. Bataillon, *Études sur le Portugal au temps de l'Humanisme* (Coimbra, 1952)

J. de Carvalho, *Estudios sobre a cultura portuguesa no século XVI* (Coimbra, 1947–8)

R. W. Chambers, *Thomas More* (London, 1935)

L. Einstein, *The Italian Renaissance in England* (New York, 1903)

J. Huizinga, *Erasmus* (New York–London, 1924)

A. Hyma, *The Youth of Erasmus* (Michigan, 1930)

S. Jayne, *John Colet and Marsilio Ficino* (Oxford, 1963)

*The New Cambridge Modern History*, vol. I, chapter V (Cambridge, 1957)

M. M. Phillips, *Erasmus and the Northern Renaissance* (London, 1949)

A. Renaudet, *Préreforme et Humanisme à Paris pendant les Guerres d'Italie* (Paris, 1953)

A. Roersch, *L'Humanisme Belge á l'Époque de la Renaissance* (Brussels, 1910)

D. Rubio, *Classical Scholarship in Spain* (Washington, 1934)

H. Rupprich, *Humanismus und Renaissance in den deutschen Stadten und Universitaten* (Leipsic, 1938)

F. Seebohm, *The Oxford Reformers* (London, 1887)

R. B. Tate, *Joan Margarit i Pau Cardinal-Bishop of Gerona* (Manchester, 1955)

A. A. Tilley, *The French Renaissance* (London, 1919)

R. Weiss, *Humanism in England during the Fifteenth Century* (Oxford, 1957)

R. Weiss, 'Italian Humanism in Western Europe' in *Italian*

BIBLIOGRAPHY

*Renaissance Studies—A Tribute to the late Cecilia M. Ady* edited by E. F. Jacob (London, 1960)

Chapter 8

L. Baldacci, *Il petrarchismo italiano del Cinquecento* (Milan–Naples, 1957)

E. Casady, *Henry Howard Earl of Surrey* (New York, 1938)

E. K. Chambers, *Sir Thomas Wyatt and other Studies* (London, 1933)

J. G. Fucilla, *Estudios sobre el Petrarquismo en España* (Madrid, 1960)

H. Gambier, *Italie et Pétrarchisme poetique en France* (Padua, 1936)

O. Hietsch, *Die Petrarcaubersetzungen Sir Thomas Wyatts* (Vienna, 1960)

H. Keniston, *Garcilaso de la Vega* (New York, 1922)

A. Krause, *Jorge Manrique and the Cult of Death in Cuatrocientos* (Berkeley, Cal., 1937)

A. Meozzi, *Lirica della Rinascita italiana in Spagna e Portogallo nei secoli XV-XVII* (Firenze, 1942)

A. Pagès, *Ausias March et ses prédecesseurs* (Paris, 1912)

J. Vianey, *Le Pétrarquisme en France au XVI* siècle* (Montpellier, 1909)


Chapter 9

M. Bataillon, *La Célestine selon Fernando de Rojas* (Paris, 1961)

E. J. Eckardt, *Studien zur deutschen Bühnengeschichte der Renaissance* (Leipsic, 1931)

E. Forsyth, *La tragédie française de Jodelle à Corneille (1553–1640)—Le thème de la vengeance* (Paris, 1962)

W. W. Greg, *Pastoral Poetry and Pastoral Drama* (London, 1906)

J. Haassen, *Drama und Theater der Humanistenschulen in Deutschland* (Augsburg, 1929)

A. Hulubei, *L'Eclogue en France au XVI* siècle* (Paris, 1938)

J. S. Kennard, *The Italian Theatre*, vol. I (New York, 1932)

R. Lebegue, *La tragédie française de la Renaissance* (Brussels, 1944)

H. McCusker, *John Bale, Dramatist and Antiquary* (Bryn Mawr, 1942)

M. Mignon, *Études sur le Theatre Français de la Renaissance* (Paris, 1923)

A. Nicoll, *The English Theatre* (London, 1936)

A. W. Reed, *Early Tudor Drama* (London, 1936)

E. Rigal, *De Jodelle a Moliére* (Paris, 1911)


*Chapter 10*

A. Albertazzi, *Il Romanzo* (Milan, 1902)

P. Jourda, *Marguerite d'Angoulême Duchesse d'Alençon, Reine de Navarre (1492–1549)* (Paris, 1930)

J. Plattard, *The Life of François Rabelais* (London, 1930)

H. A. Rennert, *The Spanish Pastoral Romances* (Philadelphia, 1912)

# Index

# INDEX